BibleTelling
Old Testament Survey

Book 4
John Walsh

◆ Copyright © 2024 by John and Jan Walsh ◆
Edition 1.1

Published by BibleTelling

All rights reserved. No part of this publication may be reproduced, distributed, or transmitted in any form without the prior written permission of the publisher. For permission requests, email: info@BibleTelling.com

Permission is granted for making copies of certain pages, as specified in lesson instructions, and for Tests at the end of the book.

Author ‑ John Walsh
Cover Design ‑ Joe Horine, Normal, IL
Front Cover Photo ‑ Robert Shaw, Heyworth, IL
Project Manager ‑ Roger Schmidgall, BibleTelling Administrator
Academic Content Creator ‑ Jan Walsh
Editorial Consultant ‑ Brent Walsh

Websites and Resources

BibleTelling.org ‑ Events and services, including Holy Land seminars, training, and free download of *All the Stories of the Bible*

Story-of-the-Day Subscription: The whole Bible in a year — one story at a time.

BTStories.com ‑ free online access to audio, video, text, timeline, map, and insights for *All the Stories of the Bible*

Mobile App ‑ **BT Stories** in the Apple, Android, and Windows App stores

LanguageOlympics.org ‑ Literacy and ESL training using Bible stories

BibleTelling
Old Testament Survey - Book 4

Table of Contents

BibleTelling	4
Storyboards - Techniques for Learning Stories	5
Lesson 28 - Solomon	7
Lesson 29 - Naaman	15
Lesson 30 - Four Lepers	23
Lesson 31 - Jonah	31
Lesson 32 - The King of Assyria	39
Lesson 33 - Jeremiah	47
Lesson 34 - Daniel	55
Lesson 35 - Returning to Jerusalem	63
Lesson 36 - Esther	71

TESTS for Lessons 28 – 36   End of Book

BibleTelling

BibleTelling is a powerful way of communicating God's truth. It uses Bible stories, which are told in a simple way without embellishing. The stories are accurate to Scripture and are presented in a conversational style — a 'telling format.' With this course, you will learn to tell Bible stories naturally, without memorizing the words of the stories. They should be told the same way people tell what they had for breakfast. They see the breakfast in their minds and tell what they see.

Can anyone do this?

It is true that some people can simply read the story and then tell it. But most people need help remembering the essential parts of a story. This is a skill anyone can develop. On the facing page are some methods used in BibleTelling. We have found that each person will eventually find their favorite way of learning Bible stories. This may be listening, outlining, dramatizing, creating art, poetry, music, etc.

First Step

There are many methods of learning a Bible story, but they all have the same first step. Always start the learning process by dividing the story into sections.

What are the benefits of learning Bible Stories?

The Scriptural command is clear: "Hide God's word in your heart." Memorizing verses is one way to accomplish this, but it leaves a vast amount of the Bible untouched. 75% of Scripture was written as stories. These can easily be learned and told to others.

Learning these stories opens a person's understanding of the Bible and brings spiritual insight. It helps a person develop strong decision-making skills. In addition, it provides new opportunities for helping others, since most people enjoy listening to Bible stories.

Procedure for each Lesson

1. Read the story as it appears in this book.
2. Read the same story in the Bible as you fill in the blanks for 'Search the Scriptures.'
3. Do the Crossword Puzzle.
4. Follow the instructions in the Storyboard section. This will help you remember the sequence of events.
5. Write your answers to the three questions at the top of the Reflections page.
6. Do at least one of the Communication Activities. This helps you internalize the truths of the story.
7. Tell the story to someone else without looking at notes. Don't think of the story as words, but as mental pictures you see and describe. This first telling is called "stumbling through the story." Don't be concerned if you forget a few things.
8. Tell the story a total of five times. This will make the story permanent in your memory.
9. Discuss the story with someone else or with a group of people. The Group Discussion questions will get you started, but the dialogue will quickly inspire additional thoughts. This activity greatly enhances a person's understanding of the Biblical event.

Experience for yourself the power of a Bible story simply told!

Storyboards ~ Techniques for Learning Stories
Learning stories without memorizing words

A storyboard is a graphic organizer that helps you visualize the different sections of a story. There are several types of storyboards. Here are some that work especially well with BibleTelling.

Draw and Tell

This involves drawing stick figures, lines, arrows, circles, etc. Once this is done, you can look at your pictures and remember the various parts of the story. This also helps you recall the story in the future. It is easier to remember pictures than memorized words. When you can see the story in your mind, you can easily share it with others! Each lesson has a page for drawing the storyboard.

Location Method

This is a 'Walk and Tell' exercise. It is a storyboard technique that involves moving around in a physical location. This can be a living room, bedroom, classroom, office, or an outdoor space. Using this method, you assign various parts of your story to spots around the room. At each spot, look around for objects that remind you of details in that part of the story — furniture, pictures, lights, chairs, tables, etc. This memory activity uses a person's large muscles, so it is important to physically walk to each location as you tell the story.

Once you choose a room, it is important not to stand in one location and simply point around the room. Instead, walk and tell the story as you move from one location to another. Also, no one spot should take over too much of the story. Keep moving.

'Mind Palace'

This is a mental exercise. Think of an area that is familiar to you — a place you could walk through with your eyes closed. Mentally follow the route and assign parts of the story to various spots along the way. By moving through this space in your mind, you will remember the information you have associated with each place along the path.

Hand Motions and Facial Expressions

This method is especially effective for learning a story that has a list in it — like the seven days of Creation, the ten plagues of Egypt, the Ten Commandments, etc. It is also good for learning a story that is mostly a conversation.

Your brain is good at remembering patterns that involve physical movement of your hands and body. This includes hand motions and facial expressions.

As you are learning a set of hand motions, make sure each movement leads you into the next one. Don't drop your hands and then start the next motion. This causes a memory break. Instead, move from one motion to another. Once you learn a set of hand motions, repeat them several times until you develop 'muscle memory.' We have put suggested hand motions in several of the stories in this book. NOTE: You will <u>not</u> use these hand movements when you are actually telling the story to your listeners.

Layering

Another helpful idea is to think of the story in terms of 'layers.' First, arrange the essential parts of the story according to the order in which they happened. Then go back and add new information to each part. Every layer enriches the story.

Introduction to Lesson 28

King Solomon is celebrated for his wisdom, wealth, and the construction of God's Temple. His life is a fascinating blend of triumph and tragedy.

He was best known for his exceptional wisdom, which was a gift from God. His greatest accomplishment was the construction of the Temple.

David had conquered all the nations along the key trade route that connected civilizations to the north and south of Israel. By taxing the trade caravans, he amassed significant wealth and power. Solomon then sustained this vast empire and expanded its extensive trade with other nations

Despite his early successes, Solomon's later years were stained by idolatry and a decline in his moral character. This led to his kingdom being divided after his death.

Lesson 28 – Solomon
I Kings 3, 4, 6, 8, 9, 10   II Chronicles 1-7

Solomon Asks for Wisdom

Before David died, he made his son Solomon king of Israel. Solomon loved the Lord and tried to follow the example of his father. One day, the Lord appeared to him in a dream and asked, "What do you want me to give you?"

The young king answered without hesitation. "Lord, my father was a great king. I feel like a child who doesn't know anything. Yet, you have placed me over your great people. Please give me the understanding to rule them wisely."

The Lord was pleased with Solomon's answer. "You have asked for wisdom instead of long life, riches, or peace. Therefore, I will give you wisdom like no one has ever had or ever will have. In addition, I will also give you riches and honor. And, if you continue to follow me like your father did, I will also give you long life."

Solomon Uses Wisdom

Soon after this promise, two women came before Solomon with a complaint against each other. One said, "This woman and I live in the same house. I gave birth to a son, and three days later she gave birth to a son. While we were sleeping, she accidentally rolled over on her baby and killed him. In the night, she discovered what she had done. So she took my child from beside me and put her dead son in his place.

When I awoke in the morning to nurse my son, the child was dead. I then realized it was not my son at all, but hers. She has my child."

The other woman said, "No, the living child is mine and the dead one is hers!" The two began arguing in front of the king.

He turned to a guard and said, "Come here with a sword." Then pointing to the child, he said, "Divide the child in two and give each mother a half."

One woman cried out, "No, don't kill my son! She can have him! Please let him live."

The other woman said, "Yes, cut the child in half, so we both will have a part."

The king turned to the guard, "Give the child to the first woman. I know she is the mother because her heart cries out for the child."

When Israel heard this story, they knew God had given Solomon great wisdom. Over the years, his wisdom increased and he wrote thousands of proverbs and songs.

Solomon's fame spread throughout all the surrounding nations. People traveled long distances to hear his expertise about nature — trees, animals, birds, reptiles, and fish.

Solomon Builds the Temple

The king knew it was his responsibility to build the House of the Lord. So he assembled a workforce, brought cedar wood from Lebanon, and had men quarry large stones and shape them for the foundation.

He began constructing the Temple 480 years after Israel's exodus from Egypt, and the entire project took seven years to complete.

There were no sounds of tools at the Temple site because everything was cut and crafted away from the building area. Once the Temple was completed, the interior walls were entirely paneled with cedar, and the inner sanctuary was overlaid with pure gold.

King Solomon assembled all the leaders from each tribe of Israel, and the Ark of God was moved into the 'Most Holy Place' inside the inner sanctuary. Suddenly, the glory of the Lord filled the Temple like a cloud. God's presence was so awesome that the priests could not fulfill their duties.

The king faced the people and blessed them, and then he gave a prayer of dedication to the Lord. When all was done, the people praised the Lord and returned to their homes.

God met with Solomon a second time and said, "I have sanctified the house you built for me, and I will establish your kingdom forever if you will continue to walk with me as your father did. But if you or your sons depart from me, and disobey my commandments, I will take Israel off from this land, I will depart from this temple, and it will become a heap and a disgrace."

Solomon ruled over Israel and became greater than all the kings on earth in riches and wisdom. The people lived in peace all the years that Solomon was king.

Search the Scriptures 28 – Solomon
I Kings 3, 4, 6, 8, 9, 10 • II Chronicles 1-7

1. God appeared to Solomon in a dream and said, "_____ for what you want me to _____ you." (3:5)
2. Solomon asked for a/an _____ heart to rule the Lord's people. (3:9)
3. The Lord was _____ that Solomon asked for this. (3:10)
4. The Lord said, "I will also give you what you have _____ asked, both _____ and honor . . . and if you will walk in my ways, keeping my statutes and my _____, as your father David walked, then I will _____ your days." (3:13-14)
5. Two _____ came to Solomon about two _____, one dead and the other alive. (3:16-22)
6. When they _____ claimed the living child, Solomon said, "Bring me a _____." (3:23-24)
7. Then he commanded, "Divide the living child in _____ and give _____ to each woman." (3:25)
8. The first woman cried out, "Don't _____ him!" The other woman said, "Yes, _____ him so we will both have a half." The king said, "Give the _____ child to the first woman — she is the _____." (3:24-27)
9. All Israel saw that the _____ of God was in Solomon. (3:28)
10. All the years of Solomon's reign, he had _____ on every side. (4:24)
11. Solomon's wisdom and understanding caused his _____ to spread throughout all the surrounding _____. He wrote three thousand _____ and more than a thousand songs. (4:29-32)
12. He also knew all about trees, animals, _____, reptiles, and fish. People and kings from other nations came to _____ Solomon speak. (4:33-34)
13. Solomon began to build the Temple _____ years after the Israelites came out of the land of Egypt. (6:1)
14. No hammers, chisels, or other _____ were heard in the temple while it was being built. (6:7)
15. The inside walls were made of _____, and the floors were made of cypress. (6:15)
16. Solomon made an inner sanctuary for the Ark of God and covered it with pure _____. (6:19-20)
17. Solomon's Temple took _____ years to build. (6:38)
18. Solomon called together all the elders of Israel, and the priests brought the _____ of God from the Tabernacle where it had been kept, and they set it in the 'Most Holy Place' in the inner sanctuary. (8:1-7)
19. When the priests came out of the Most Holy Place, a _____ filled the House of the Lord. (8:10)
20. Then King Solomon _____ the whole assembly of Israel. (8:14)
21. When Solomon finished building the temple, the Lord appeared to him a _____ time and said: "If you will do all that I command, your kingdom will be established _____. (9:4-5)
22. But if you turn away from me and serve other _____, then I will take Israel off their _____. (9:7)
23. I will reject this temple and _____ myself from it. It will be in ruins and disgrace. People who pass by will ask, '_____ has the Lord done such a thing to this temple?'" (9:8)
24. People will answer, 'Because they have turned _____ from the Lord their God who brought their ancestors out of _____ and have worshiped _____ gods. That is why the _____ brought all this disaster on them.'" (9:9)

Crossword 28 – Solomon

Use these words:
animals, Ark, ask, cedar, child, commandments, David, dream, forever, gold, kill, land, living, nations, proverbs, riches, seven, Solomon, sword, tabernacle, temple, tools, understanding, wisdom

ACROSS

2 - Solomon said, "I feel like a little ___."
8 - There were no sounds of ___ at the temple site while it was being built.
9 - Solomon was very knowledgeable about trees, ___, birds, reptiles, and fish.
10 - The Ark of God had been kept in the ___ for many years.
12 - Each of two women claimed that the ___ baby was hers.
13 - Solomon wrote thousands of ___ and songs.
16 - The priests put the ___ of God in the sanctuary of the Temple.
18 - The inside walls of the temple were covered with this type of wood.
21 - The Lord promised Solomon long life if he would keep God's ___.
22 - To end the argument between two women, the king asked for a ___.
23 - It took ___ years to build the temple.
24 - The Temple's inner sanctuary was covered in pure ___.

DOWN

1 - Another name for the House of the Lord
3 - God spoke to Solomon in a ___.
4 - Solomon asked God to give him ___ to rule the Lord's people.
5 - God said if Solomon would obey him his kingdom would be established ___.
6 - The king gave the living child to the mother who cried out, "Don't ___ him!"
7 - The name of King Solomon's father
11 - All of Israel saw that the ___ of God was in Solomon.
14 - Solomon's fame spread throughout all the surrounding ___.
15 - People came from all over to hear ___ speak.
17 - God promised to give Solomon both ___ and honor.
19 - God said if the Israelites turned away from him, they would be taken off their ___.
20 - God told Solomon to ___ for whatever he wanted.

Storyboard 28 ~ Solomon

Section 1 ~ Solomon Asks for Wisdom

Use a combination of hand movements and drawings to remember this section.

👉 **Start with the hand motions to remember Solomon's conversation with God.**
- point right to his father *(a great king)*
- other hand point to self *(like a child)*
- hold both hands out to the nation of Israel *(great people)*
- both hands next to head *(understanding)*
- both hands around a smile *(God is pleased)*

▶ **In the first box on the next page, draw what Solomon did <u>not</u> ask for.**
- For long life, draw a long line with a baby at one end and an old man at the other.
- For riches and peace, draw a $ under the line, and the wings of a dove
- God gave him wisdom and long life, but with conditions.
  (Draw a circle around 'long life' to indicate God's conditions.)

Section 2 ~ Solomon Uses Wisdom

The event about the two mothers is "a story within a story." It is easy to remember.
The end of this section describes Solomon increasing in wisdom.

▶ **Draw five small icons in the second box to help to remember these details.**
- The people knew God had given wisdom to the king.
- He increased in wisdom over the years.
- He wrote proverbs and songs.
- People traveled to Israel to hear him speak.
- God gave Solomon great wealth.

Section 3 ~ Solomon Builds the Temple

The events that surround the building of the Temple can be divided into three happenings:
(1) construction of the Temple (2) dedication service (3) God's serious conversation with Solomon.

▶ **Draw a few icons in the third box to remember these three events.**

(1) Concerning the construction, envision the king selecting a work crew. They pick up wood and big stones. Behind them is the number 480 (years since leaving Egypt). In front is the number 7 (years of construction). They work quietly, then put the wood and gold inside.

(2) To remember the dedication, envision the leaders getting together as the Ark goes into the Temple. The Glory of the Lord comes down and the priests must stop their work. The king blesses the people and gives a prayer of dedication.

(3) God's serious conversation with Solomon has two positive aspects and three negative consequences.

<u>Two positive aspects</u>
(+) I have sanctified the Temple.
(+) I will establish your kingdom if you obey.

<u>Three negative consequences</u> (If you or your sons don't obey)
(−) I will take Israel off the land.
(−) I will leave the Temple.
(−) The Temple will become a heap and a disgrace.

Drawing Storyboard 28 ~ Solomon
Using the boxes below, show the storyboard in pictures, symbols, or words.

Solomon Asks for Wisdom

Solomon Uses Wisdom

Solomon Builds the Temple

Reflection – 28

- What was your favorite part of the story? Tell why.
  _____

- What did you learn about people from the story of *Solomon*?
  _____

- What did you learn about God from the story of *Solomon*?
  _____

Communication Activities
Communicate the story in your most enjoyable form of expression.

- **Art:** Paint (or draw) a picture of Solomon telling the guard to divide the baby.
- **Storytelling:** Tell the Temple dedication story in the first person, as if you just arrived home from the service and you're telling a neighbor all about it. Include what you heard about the two women and the baby.
- **Impromptu Coffee Shop Drama:** Three friends meet in a coffee shop. Two have just returned from Jerusalem, and they excitedly share their experience of the Temple dedication with the third, who eagerly asks for more details. The impromptu answers infuse the story with insight and personal experience.
- **Music:** Craft a song that retells this story in music.
- **Poetry:** Craft a poem about Solomon judging the conflict between the two women.
- **Interview:** Enlist several volunteers to be on a Biblical panel. Each is to stay 'in character' during the interview. The panel includes Solomon, a builder, a priest, mother #1, mother #2, and everyone in the audience as attendees of the dedication service. Ask several questions to each person on the panel and the audience. Finally, allow your audience to ask questions to those on the panel.
- **News Report:** Write an article of this story as if it is from the ancient *Jerusalem Times*. Look up the Scriptures (*I Kings 3-10; II Chronicles 1-7*) for more details.
- **Research:** Study what is known about the First Temple built by Solomon. Report your findings to the group.

Student has completed one or more of the communication activities.   Teacher initials _____

Banner or Bumper Sticker: Give the essence of this story in seven words or less.

_____

Tell the story: To whom did you tell the story, and what was their response?

_____
_____

Group Discussion - 28

Solomon

1. If God offered to give you anything you wanted, what would you ask for, and why?

2. What does it mean to have wisdom today, and how can we seek it in our daily lives?

3. God gave a strict warning to Solomon regarding faithfulness. How does this relate to our choices in life? What are the consequences of <u>not</u> having wisdom?

4. What do you think it means to walk with God in today's world? How can we remain faithful amid distractions and challenges?

5. Optional: The glory of the Lord filling the Temple was a powerful experience for the people. Have you felt God's presence in a powerful way?

NOTES:

Introduction to Lesson 29

After King Solomon died, a civil war broke out and his kingdom divided into two nations. The one in the north was called the Kingdom of Israel, and the one in the south was called the Kingdom of Judah. The descendants of David ruled over Judah.

Naaman, although he was a Syrian, is one of only five men in the Bible referred to as a 'mighty man of valor.' He is the only one who was a Gentile. The rest were from Judah or Israel. They include Jephthah, Gideon, David, and Jeroboam.

Because of Naaman's many victories in battle, the king of Syria highly respected and valued him as an army commander. Still, the Scriptures say that it was the Lord who gave him those victories.

Lesson 29 – Naaman
II Kings 5:1-27

Naaman was the great commander of the Syrian army. During one of their wars with Israel, he captured a young girl and brought her back to be a servant for his wife.

In time, Naaman realized he had leprosy, a crippling disease of the skin. The young slave girl said, "I wish my master could go to Israel. They have a prophet who can heal people, even those with leprosy."

Naaman told this to the king. Immediately, the king made preparations to send Naaman to the king of Israel. He sent gifts of gold, silver, and fine clothes along with a letter saying, "I'm sending my servant Naaman so you can cure him of leprosy."

The king of Israel was shocked when he read the letter. He ripped his clothes and yelled, "Who does he think I am? I'm not God. I can't cure people of leprosy! I know what he's doing. He's trying to start a war with me."

Elisha heard about this and sent a message to the king. "Why are you ripping your clothes? Send the man to me so he'll know there's a prophet in Israel."

So Naaman and his men rode to the prophet's house and stood outside. Elisha sent a messenger out who said, "Go down to the Jordan River and wash seven times. After you're done, you'll be healed of leprosy."

Naaman was furious when he heard this and stormed away. He said, "A true prophet would come out and stand in front of me. He'd pray to the Lord and wave his hand over my skin. If I thought washing in a river would help, I'd bathe in one of the beautiful rivers of Damascus — not a dirty river like the Jordan."

His servants said to him, "If the prophet had asked you to do something hard, you would've done it. But he told you to do something easy — wash and be clean."

So Naaman went to the Jordan River and dipped down into it seven times. Suddenly his skin was healed just as the prophet said it would be. In fact, it was like the skin of a young boy.

After Naaman was healed at the Jordan River, he and his men went back to the prophet's house and stood before him. Naaman said, "Today I've learned that there's no god on earth except the God of Israel. Please accept my humble gift."

Elisha said, "As sure as God lives, I won't take a gift from you." Naaman insisted, but the prophet still refused.

Then the commander said, "Please let me have as much soil as two mules can carry. I'll no longer worship any other god. Instead, I'll kneel on this soil from Israel and worship the Lord God."

Shortly after Naaman left, Gehazi said to himself, *My master let this Syrian off too easy. He should have paid something. I'll catch up with him and ask for a gift for myself.*

So Gehazi went after the Syrian commander. Soon, Naaman saw him coming and stopped his chariot. He got off and greeted the servant. "Is everything all right?"

Gehazi said, "Yes, everything is fine. My master just found out that two guests are staying with us tonight. He was wondering if you would like to help with the expenses — possibly 75 pounds of silver and a couple of sets of clothes."

"Certainly! Here, I'll give you 150 pounds of silver in two bags, as well as two sets of clothes." The commander gave this to a couple of his men so they could carry it back for the servant.

Gehazi had the men take the silver and clothes to his own house. Once everything was put away, he sent the men away. He then went and stood next to his master.

Elisha said, Gehazi, where did you go?"

"I didn't go anywhere."

Elisha said, "Oh my dear friend. My spirit was there when Naaman stopped his chariot and stepped down to greet you. It wasn't your place to accept anything for yourself. Therefore, Naaman's leprosy is now attaching itself to your skin."

With that, Gehazi turned and left the house. He looked down at his arms, and they were already white with leprosy.

Search the Scriptures 29 – Naaman
II Kings 5:1-27

1. Naaman was the commander of the _____ army. He was greatly valued by the King of Syria because of his leadership in gaining victory over Israel's army. But Naaman was a _____. (5:1)
2. After one of their battles, the Syrians captured a young _____ in Israel and brought her to be a servant for Naaman's _____. The girl said to her mistress, "I wish my master could go to the _____ in Samaria. He would _____ him of his leprosy." (5:2-3)
3. Naaman told this to his king. Immediately, the king said, "_____ now, and I will send a _____ to the king of Israel." So Naaman went, taking the letter, plus many gifts. (5:4-5)
4. The letter said: "When you receive this letter, you will know that I have sent to you _____, my servant, so you can cure him of his _____." (5:6)
5. Then the king of Israel tore his _____ and said, "I'm not God and I can't cure people from leprosy! The king of Syria is trying to start a _____ against me." (5:7)
6. _____, the prophet, heard about this and sent a message to the king. "Why are you ripping your clothes? Send the man to _____ and he will _____ there's a prophet in Israel." (5:8)
7. So Naaman and his men came with their horses and _____ and stood at the _____ of the prophet's house. Elisha sent a _____ out saying, "Go and wash in the _____ River seven times and you will be healed." (5:9-10)
8. But Naaman was _____ and turned and left, saying, "I _____ he would come out and stand and call on the name of the Lord his God and _____ his hand over me and cure me. Aren't the rivers of _____ better than all the waters of Israel? Could I not wash in them and be healed?" So he went away in a _____. (5:11-12)
9. His servants asked, "If the prophet had told you to do some _____ thing, wouldn't you have done it? But he told you simply '_____ and be clean.'" So Naaman went and dipped himself _____ times in the Jordan, and he was healed. His skin was like that of a young _____. (5:13-14)
10. Then Naaman and his men went back to the prophet's house and _____ before him. Naaman said, "I know that there is _____ god on earth except the God of _____. Now, accept a gift from me." (5:15)
11. Elisha said, "As sure as God lives, I will _____ accept a gift from you." Naaman insisted, but the prophet still _____. Then Naaman said, "Please let me have as much _____ as two mules can carry. From now on, I will no longer _____ any other god. Instead, I'll kneel on this soil from Israel and worship the _____ God." (5:16-17)
12. After Naaman left, Gehazi said to himself, *"My master should have accepted a gift from that man. I'll run after him and _____ something from him."* (5:20)
13. _____ saw him running after him, so he stopped his chariot, got _____ and asked, "Is all well?" Gehazi said, "Yes, all is _____. My master has sent me to say that just now, _____ guests have arrived. Please give them some _____ and two changes of clothing." (5:21-22)
14. Naaman gave even more than was asked and had two of his _____ carry it back to the house of Gehazi. (5:23-24)
15. After _____ sent the men away, he went and stood in front of his _____. Elisha asked, "Where did you go?" Gehazi answered, "I went _____." (5:25)
16. Elisha said, "Didn't my _____ go with you when Naaman got down from his chariot to meet you? Therefore, Naaman's _____ will now be on you." (5:26-27)

Crossword 29 - Naaman

Use these words:
child, clothes, commander, Damascus, door, Gehazi, gift, God, great, Jordan, leper, leprosy, letter messenger, nowhere, prophet, refused, silver, soil, Syrians, wash, wave, white, wife

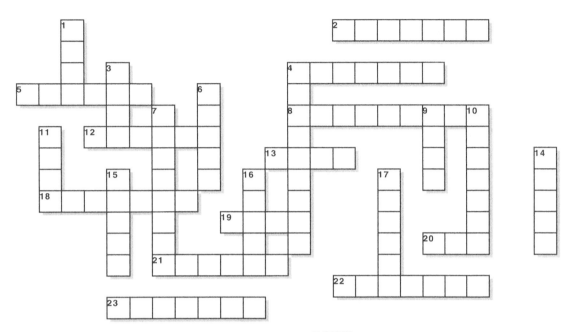

ACROSS

2 - Elisha said, "Send the man to me and he will know there is a ___ in Israel."

4 - When the king of Israel read the letter, he tore his ___.

5 - Naaman was told to go and wash seven times in the ___ River.

8 - Elisha sent a ___ to talk with Naaman at the door.

12 - ___ ran after Naaman's chariot.

13 - Elisha's message was simply, "___ and be clean."

18 - A young girl said Naaman could go to the prophet in Israel and be cured of his ___.

19 - The girl was the servant of Naaman's ___.

20 - Naaman said, "I know there is no god on earth except the ___ of Israel."

21 - Naaman took large amounts of ___, gold, and expensive clothing on his trip.

22 - The ___ captured a young girl in Israel.

23 - When Elisha asked, "Where did you go?" his servant said, "I went ___."

DOWN

1 - Naaman and his men came to Elisha's house and stood at the ___.

3 - Naaman thought the prophet would come and ___ his hand over him and cure him.

4 - Naaman was the ___ of the Syrian army.

6 - After Naaman obeyed Elisha's instructions, his skin became like that of a young ___.

7 - Naaman said the rivers of ___ were better than all the waters in Israel.

9 - Gehazi thought his master should have accepted a ___ from Naaman.

10 - Naaman wanted to give a gift to Elisha, but the prophet ___.

11 - Naaman asked for as much ___ as two mules could carry.

14 - Naaman was a ___ - he had the disease of leprosy.

15 - Naaman's servants asked, "If the prophet had told you do some ___ thing, wouldn't you have done it?"

16 - After Gehazi lied to the prophet, his skin turned ___ with leprosy.

17 - The king of Syria sent a ___ to the king of Israel.

Storyboard 29 – Naaman

Section 1 – Two Kings

Location Method: This section involves five people, so it is perfect for placing the story around a room. Choose places for the following:

- Naaman
- The servant girl
- The king of Syria
- The king of Israel
- Elisha
- Gehazi

At each location, find objects that remind you of what the story says about that person.

▶ On the facing page, place several drawings in the first box representing the six people and what we know about them.

Section 2 – The Healing

This section is full of actions, so it is easy to remember.

▶ **In box two, draw symbols that will remind you of these five actions:**

- Elisha's instructions
- Naaman's reaction
- Going to the river
- Gifts offered
- Taking soil from Israel

Section 3 – Gehazi's Greed

This section is a story inside a story. It is more difficult to remember because it contains two conversations and a list of items.

▶ **In the third box, create drawings to remind you of the conversations:**

- Gehazi talking to himself
- Naaman's question to Gehazi
- Gehazi lying to Naaman
- Transfer of goods
- Conversation with Elisha

Drawing Storyboard 29 ~ Naaman

Using the boxes below, show the storyboard in pictures, symbols, or words.

Two Kings

The Healing

Gehazi's Greed

Reflection - 29

- What was your favorite part of the story? Tell why.
  _____

- What did you learn about people from the story of *Naaman*?
  _____

- What did you learn about God from the story of *Naaman*?
  _____

Communication Activities
Communicate the story in your most enjoyable form of expression.

- **Art:** Paint (or draw) a picture of Naaman washing himself in the Jordan River.
- **Storytelling:** Write and tell a first-person story as if you are one of the following: the servant girl, one of Naaman's servants, or Gehazi.
- **Drama:** This story contains eight conversations between two people.
    - Naaman and the slave girl
    - The king of Syria with the king of Israel
    - The King of Israel and Elisha
    - Elisha and Naaman
    - Naaman and his servants
    - Naaman and Elisha
    - Gehazi and Naaman
    - Elisha and Gehazi

  Produce a drama performed by two people, who keep changing characters. To add a bit of humor, use various hats for the many characters.

- **Writing:** Write a news article about the events of this story from the perspective of a newspaper in ancient Syria.
- **Poetry:** Write the entire story as a poem.

Student has completed one or more of the communication activities.   Teacher initials _____

Banner or Bumper Sticker: Give the essence of this story in seven words or less.

☐

Tell the story: To whom did you tell the story, and what was their response?
_____
_____

Group Discussion - 29

Naaman

1. Naaman's view of life almost kept him from being healed. What barriers do we have in our lives that keep us from experiencing God's best for us?

2. Naaman listened to people of a lower status in society than himself — the servant girl, and his servants. Give examples of a time you were helped by unexpected sources.

3. Elisha's instructions were simple. In what ways do we overlook simple solutions to our own problems?

4. Naaman had expectations about how his healing would take place. Give examples of how our expectations limit our walk with God.

5. In what ways can this story apply to us today?

Notes:

Introduction to Lesson 30

There was a narrow strip of land in between the great desert to the east of Israel and the Mediterranean Sea to the west. All north/south traders had to use this route. The nations who occupied the land were able to collect a tariff on the goods going through their country. Therefore, every country wanted to control as much of that area as possible. This led to many wars, including the conflict in this story.

Elisha was a powerful prophet in the Northern Kingdom of Israel. His ministry began when he was anointed by Elijah to become his successor.

Elisha's ministry was during the reign of four kings of Israel. He was not only respected by the kings of Israel, but also by the king of Syria.

A person who had the disease of leprosy was called a 'leper.' By law, these people had to keep themselves separated from the general population.

In this story, four lepers sat outside the gate of the city because they were not allowed to be in the city.

Lesson 30 ~ Four Lepers
II Kings 6:24 – 7:20

The king of Syria took his army and invaded the Northern Kingdom of Israel. They surrounded the capital city of Samaria and set up camp not far from the city walls. They cut off all supplies going into the city.

Eventually there was no food, and the people started to starve. It was so bad that a donkey's head sold for two pounds of silver, and a small bowl of dove's droppings sold for two ounces of silver.

A woman saw the king walking along the top of the city wall. She asked him to help her. He said, "I don't know if I can. Tell me about your problem."

She said, "My friend won't keep her promise. We agreed we'd eat our two sons, mine on the first day and hers on the second. So, we boiled and ate my son, but now she has hidden her son."

When the king heard this, he ripped his clothes. He said, "I'll get Elisha for this if it's the last thing I do." He sent a guard to cut off the prophet's head.

Elisha was sitting in his house with several of the elders of Israel. He said, "Our murdering king has sent a guard to cut off my head. The king is right behind him."

Just then the king walked in. He yelled at the prophet. "You said all this trouble is from God. So why should I serve him if he acts like this?"

Elisha said, "I have a message for you from God. He said this disaster is almost over. Tomorrow at this time, people will buy a sack of fine flour for a few coins. They'll buy a large sack of barley for the same price."

The king's chief adviser laughed. "That's impossible! We couldn't have that much food around here even if God opened up the windows of heaven."

The man of God looked at him, and then said, "You'll see it with your own eyes, but you won't eat any of it."

That evening, as it was beginning to get dark, the Syrian army heard a loud noise like a large army marching toward them. The noise got louder and sounded like the invading army had many horses and chariots.

The Syrian soldiers thought Israel had hired other nations to come and help them. They yelled, "Let's get out of here!" They immediately ran away, leaving everything behind.

Four lepers were sitting just outside the city gates. One said to the others, "Why are we just sitting here slowly dying of hunger?"

Another one said, "Well, it's no better in the city. If we go in there, we'll still die of hunger."

"Yes, that's true, but we can't stay here. Let's go into the Syrian camp. If they kill us — well, we're about to die anyway. But maybe they'll have pity on us and give us food."

So, at twilight, the four men got up and walked toward the camp, not knowing it was empty. They went into the first tent at the edge of the camp and found food, gold, silver, and expensive clothes.

The first thing they did was eat the food. They then took the other things away and hid them. They came back and got more things from the next tent and hid them.

Finally, they said, "What we're doing isn't right. People are dying of hunger on the other side of the wall. God will punish us if we don't tell them about this." They all agreed, so they went to the city gate and yelled to the gatekeepers, telling them exactly what they found. The gatekeepers told the king's household.

When the king heard about this, he thought it was a trap. He said, "The Syrian army is hiding out of sight, waiting for us to come out of the city." To make sure, he sent a few soldiers to scout out the land. The men found the route the Syrians had taken. It was full of clothes and equipment the army had thrown away so they could run faster.

The soldiers went back and told the king what they had found. With that, people flooded out of the city to raid the Syrian camp. The price of food immediately dropped.

The king gave his chief adviser the job of crowd control at the gate. Soon, he was trampled to death. All of this fulfilled the prophet's words, "You will see it with your own eyes, but you will not eat any of it."

Search the Scriptures 30 - Four Lepers
II Kings 6:24 – 7:20

1. The king of Syria took his army and besieged Israel's capital city, _____. They set up camp close to the city walls and cut off all supplies, causing a great _____ in the city. (6:24)
2. A _____ saw the king walking along the top of the city wall. She cried out saying, "_____ me!" The king asked, "What is your _____?" (6:25-28)
3. She said, "This woman and I agreed we would _____ our two sons. We boiled and ate my _____ yesterday, but now she has _____ her son." (6:28-29)
4. When the king heard this, he ripped his clothes. He said, "May God strike me down if the head of _____ still remains on his _____ by the end of this day." (6:30-31)
5. Elisha was sitting in his house with several _____ of Israel. He said to them, "Our murdering king has sent a guard to take off my head. The king is coming right _____ him." (6:32)
6. Just then the messenger walked in. He said "This _____ is from the Lord." (6:33)
7. Elisha said, "_____ about this time, flour and barley will be sold for just shekels." (7:1)
8. The king's chief adviser (on whom the king was leaning) said to Elisha. "If the _____ himself should make _____ in heaven, could this thing really happen?" Elisha said, "You will _____ it with your own eyes, but you will not _____ any of it." (7:2)
9. Four _____ were sitting outside the _____ of the city. One said to the others, "Why are we just _____ here dying of hunger?" (7:3)
10. Another said, "If we go inside the city, there is a _____ and we will die there. If we sit here we will _____, also. So, let's go to the camp of the _____. If they spare our lives, we will _____, and if they kill us we will die." (7:4)
11. Early that evening, when the lepers got to the edge of the Syrian camp, _____ was there. (7:5)
12. Just hours before, the Lord had made the army of the Syrians hear the sound of _____ and horses — the sound of _____. They thought Israel had hired the Hittites and Egyptians to _____ them. So, just as it was starting to get dark, they ran away, leaving their tents, horses, donkeys, and everything in the camp, just as it was. They ran for their lives! (7:6-7)
13. The four men went into the first _____. They ate and drank, and carried off silver and gold and clothing and went and _____ them. Then they came back to another tent and did the same. (7:8)
14. Then, they said, "We are not doing _____ . . . Now, let us go and tell the king's household." (7:9)
15. So they went to the city _____ and yelled to the gatekeepers, telling them what they had found. (7:10)
16. The gatekeepers told the _____ household. When the _____ heard about this, he said, "The Syrians know we are _____. The army is _____ out of sight, waiting for us to come out of the city." (7:11-12)
17. So the king sent out _____ horsemen to look for the Syrian army. They saw that the route was littered with clothing and equipment the fleeing army had thrown away in their _____. (7:14-15)
18. When the messengers returned and told the king, all the _____ went out and plundered the Syrian _____. Then they had food in abundance. Flour and _____ were sold for just shekels, exactly as the Lord had declared through the prophet. (7:16)
19. The king appointed his chief adviser the job of crowd control at the _____. The people trampled on him and he died. All of this fulfilled the prophet's words, "You will see it with your own _____, but you will _____ eat any of it." (7:17)

Crossword 30 – Four Lepers

Use these words:
armies, ate, chariots, eat, Elisha, famine, food, four, gatekeepers, haste, hid, horsemen, king leper, none, right, Samaria, Syrian, trampled, trap, windows, woman

ACROSS

1 - A ___ was caused when the Syrians cut off all food supplies to Samaria.
4 - The lepers said, "We are not doing ___."
7 - The route the fleeing army took was littered with all the things they had thrown away in their ___.
10 - The lepers went and told the ___ what they had found.
11 - A ___ asked the king to solve her problem.
14 - The lepers found silver, gold, and clothing which they took and ___.
15 - The city of ___ was 'besieged' by the Syrian army
18 - The king sent two ___ to look for the Syrian army.
19 - The chief adviser said the food problem couldn't be solved even if God opened the ___ of heaven.
20 - "You will see it with your own eyes, but you will not ___ any of it."
21 - The lepers decided to go into the ___ camp.

DOWN

1 - There were ___ lepers sitting outside the gate of Samaria.
2 - The king blamed their bad situation on God's prophet, ___.
3 - God caused the Syrian army to hear the sound of ___ and horses.
5 - When the king of Samaria heard that the Syrians had deserted their camp, he thought it was a ___.
6 - When the men went into the first tent, they ___ and drank.
8 - Someone who has leprosy is called a ___.
9 - Just as the prophet predicted, the price of ___ dropped drastically.
12 - The chief adviser was ___ by crowds of Israelites rushing out the city gate.
13 - The ___ was walking along on top of the city wall.
16 - The Syrians thought the Israelites had hired other ___ to attack them.
17 - How many people were in the camp where the lepers went?

25

Storyboard 30 – Four Lepers

Section 1 – The Two Sons

▶ In the first box on the next page, draw several icons of what happened.
   IDEAS:
   - **A woman crying** – to symbolize the mother's plea to the king
   - **The king tearing his robes** – indicating his horror and despair

Section 2 – The Prophecy

▶ In the second box, draw several icons of what happened.
   IDEAS:
   - **A sack of grain and some coins** – Symbolizing the promised abundance of food
   - **A laughing man** – For the chief adviser doubting the prophecy

Section 3 – The Empty Camp

▶ In the third box, draw several icons of what happened.
   IDEAS:
   - **Running soldiers** – Symbolizing the Syrian army fleeing
   - **Gold coins and food** – Representing the wealth and provisions left behind

Section 4 – Telling the City

▶ In the fourth box, draw several icons of what happened.
   IDEAS:
   - **Four figures walking** – Representing the four lepers going to the camp
   - **A tent with an open flap** – Indicating their discovery of the empty camp
   - **A crowd rushing** – Showing the people flooding out of the city

---

Tell this story on five different occasions and you will remember it for the rest of your life.

Drawing Storyboard 30 ~ Four Lepers

Using the boxes below, show the storyboard in pictures, symbols, or words.

The Two Sons	The Prophecy

The Empty Camp	Telling the City

Reflection – 30

- What was your favorite part of the story? Tell why.
  _____

- What did you learn about people from *Four Lepers*?
  _____

- What did you learn about God from *Four Lepers*?
  _____

Communication Activities
Communicate the story in your most enjoyable form of expression.

- **Art:** Select a part of this story and paint (or draw) a picture of it.
- **Storytelling:** "Tandem Telling" is where two people take turns telling the same story. Select someone else to join you and practice telling this story in tandem. Once the two of you can easily get through the story, tell it to an audience.
- **Music:** Transform this story into a ballad that can be sung.
- **Drama:** Create a 3-minute drama featuring some Samarian citizens returning to the city after discovering the abandoned Syrian camp's food supply. Portray their emotions as they reflect on the hardships they endured during the siege and their joy at its sudden end. Highlight their gratitude toward the lepers who brought them the good news.
- **Poetry:** Write a poem that retells this story.
- **Interview:** Enlist several volunteers to be on a Biblical panel. Each is to stay 'in character' during the interview. The panel would include the king, mother #1, mother #2, Elisha, one of the lepers, a soldier in the Syrian army, and the chief advisor. Ask several questions to each person on the panel. Finally, allow your audience to ask questions to the panel.
- **News Report:** Write an article about this story as if it will appear in the ancient *Samaria Journal*. Refer to the Scriptures *(II Kings 6:24 – 7:20)* for more details.
- **Map Activity:** Draw a map highlighting three cities: Samaria (the capital of Israel), Jerusalem (the capital of Judah), and Damascus (the capital of Syria). Include the ancient boundaries of these three countries around their respective capitals.

Student has completed one or more of the communication activities.   Teacher initials _____

Banner or Bumper Sticker: Give the essence of this story in seven words or less.

Tell the story: To whom did you tell the story, and what was their response?
_____
_____

Group Discussion - 30

Four Lepers

1. The four lepers felt they had to do something about their situation. They asked the question, "What is the worst that could happen?" They then decided on the most daring option. Describe a situation where you chose the daring option.

2. The lepers were outcasts, yet God used them to save the city. Give examples of this type of thing from the Bible, history, or personal experience.

3. The prophecy in this story seemed impossible at the time. In your walk with God, what promises in the Bible did you have a hard time believing?

4. Guilt is usually considered a negative emotion, yet guilt kept the lepers from keeping their good news to themselves. When does guilt become a positive force in our lives?

5. How can we apply the lessons from this story to our own lives?

Notes:

Introduction to Lesson 31

The Prophet Jonah lived in the Northern Kingdom of Israel near the area that later became known as Galilee.

Jonah's reluctance to go to Nineveh had nothing to do with fear. Being a prophet, he knew that the Assyrians would eventually destroy his country.

The exact location of Tarshish is unknown. This was either Spain, Portugal, or the British Isles. It was as far as Jonah could go in the opposite direction of Nineveh. Still, he knew the dangers involved in getting there. The Mediterranean Sea was prone to sudden and violent storms, which often sank ships, killing everyone on board.

When Jonah visited Nineveh, it was the capital of the Assyrian Empire and the largest city in the world. The people of Nineveh worshiped the goddess of the fish. They probably heard that Jonah came to them by way of a fish, which made them eager to hear what he had to say.

The town of Joppa is a port on the Mediterranean Sea and it is a major tourist attraction today. It is now called 'Jaffa' and is a suburb of Tel Aviv in Israel.

Lesson 31 – Jonah
The Book of Jonah

The Lord said to Jonah the prophet, "Leave and go to Nineveh. Tell them I'm going to judge them because of their wickedness."

Jonah knew that God was merciful and would forgive Nineveh if they repented. But they were enemies of Israel, and Jonah didn't want to help them. So he went the opposite direction to a seaport town called Joppa. He bought a ticket and got on a ship going to Tarshish.

Once they were out at sea, God sent a violent storm. The sailors were terrified because the storm was about to break up their ship! They threw their cargo overboard to lighten the load. It didn't help, so the sailors started praying to their various gods. While all of this was going on, Jonah was fast asleep down inside the ship.

The captain went and woke him up and said, "How can you sleep? We are about to die! Get up and pray to your god."

Eventually the sailors figured out that Jonah was the reason for their troubles. They said, "Who are you, and what have you done?"

He said, "I serve the Lord God, who made the sea and the dry ground. I'm running away from him."

They yelled, "What can we do to calm the storm?"

"God only wants one thing, and the storm won't stop until he gets it. You're to grab me and throw me overboard."

The men didn't want to kill an innocent man, so they worked hard to get to land, but the storm grew worse.

Finally, they realized they couldn't fight against God. They cried out to the Lord and asked forgiveness for what they were about to do.

They then took hold of Jonah and threw him overboard. Immediately, the storm stopped. The men were amazed! They bowed down, worshiped the Lord, and promised to serve only the one true God.

As soon as Jonah went into the water, a large fish swallowed him. Jonah stayed in the fish's stomach for three days.

Finally, he prayed. "I'll do what you want me to do." With that, the fish vomited him onto the shore. Then Jonah obeyed God and went to Nineveh. When he arrived, he began walking through the city shouting, "God is going to destroy this city in 40 days!"

The people heard Jonah preach and believed what he said was true. They put on sackcloth and started to fast. They prayed and asked God to be merciful to them.

Even the king stepped down from his throne and laid aside his royal robes. He put on sackcloth and sat on a pile of ashes. He sent out a law that said, "No one is to taste any food or water. That includes animals as well. Everyone is to wear sackcloth and stop doing evil. Maybe God will change his mind and allow us to live."

The Lord saw all they were doing and knew they had turned away from their wickedness. Therefore, he stopped the judgment that was about to come upon them. Jonah was furious when he heard this! He said, "That's why I ran away and didn't come here. Kill me right now. I don't want to live."

He went to the east side of the city and made a small shelter so he could sit and see exactly what God was going to do with the city. While he was sitting there, God caused a vine to grow up next to him that provided shade from the hot sun. Jonah was pleased.

The next morning, God caused a worm to kill the vine. When the sun got hot, the plant withered. Then an east wind made the sun feel even hotter. Jonah missed having the vine, so he yelled, "I don't want to live anymore. I want to die!"

God said, "Is it right to be angry about the vine?"

"Yes, it's right for me to be angry. I'm so mad that I want to die!"

The Lord said, "You're angry because of a simple vine. You didn't plant it. You didn't water it. It came up one day and died the next. Shouldn't I also care about the people of this city? After all, there are over 120,000 children living here, not to mention all the animals."

Search the Scriptures 31 – Jonah
The Book of Jonah

1. The word of the _____ came to Jonah, "Go to the city of _____ and preach against its wickedness." But _____ went away from the presence of the Lord and headed the opposite direction. He went down to _____ and found a _____ that was going to Tarshish. (1:1-3)
2. Then the Lord sent a great _____ on the sea that caused a _____ — so strong that the ship threatened to break up. All the sailors were afraid and each one cried out to his own _____. They threw their _____ into the sea to lighten the ship. (1:4)
3. But Jonah had gone down in the _____ part of the ship and fell fast _____. The captain went and found him and said, "How can you sleep? _____ and pray to your god!" (1:5-6)
4. The _____ came to Jonah and said, "Tell us about yourself." Jonah answered, "I worship the Lord, the God of _____ . . . who made the _____ and the dry land." (1:7)
5. They asked, "What can we _____ to make the sea calm?" Jonah said, "Pick me up and throw me into the _____, and it will become calm." They did not want to be punished for harming an _____ man. But, finally they picked up Jonah and _____ him into the sea. The storm immediately _____. (1:11-15)
6. Then the men greatly feared the Lord and offered a _____ to him. (1:16)
7. The Lord caused a huge _____ to swallow Jonah, and he was in the belly of the fish _____ days and three nights. (1:17)
8. Jonah _____. to the Lord his God from inside the fish. (2:1)
9. The Lord spoke to the fish, and it _____ Jonah out onto the dry land. (2:10)
10. Then the word of the Lord came to Jonah a _____ time. "Go to Nineveh and preach the _____ I give you." (3:1-2)
11. Jonah _____ and went to Nineveh as God had told him. As he walked through the city, he shouted, "In _____ more days Nineveh will be destroyed." The people _____ God and declared a _____ . All of them put on _____. (3:3-5)
12. When God _____ what they did and how they turned from their _____ ways, he relented and did _____ bring on them the _____ he had threatened. (3:10)
13. But Jonah became _____. He prayed to the Lord, "Isn't this what I said, Lord when I was still in my _____? That is why I tried to run away to Tarshish. I knew that you are a _____ God . . . slow to _____ and abounding in _____. (4:1-2)
14. Now, Lord, take away my _____ , for it is better for me to _____ than to live." The Lord asked, "Is it _____ for you to be _____?" (4:3-4)
15. Jonah went out and _____ down at a place east of the city. There he made himself a _____, sat in its shade and waited to see what would happen to the _____. (4:5)
16. Then the Lord God made a _____ to grow up over Jonah to give him _____ . . . and Jonah was very _____ to have the plant. But the next _____, God caused a _____ to chew the plant so that it _____. (4:6-7)
17. Again Jonah said, "It is _____ for me to die than to _____." (4:8)
18. God asked Jonah, "Is it right for you to be _____ about the plant?" "It is," he said. The Lord said to Jonah, "You care about this plant, although you did not take care of it or make it _____. It came up one night and died the next _____. Should I not care for the city of Nineveh, in which there are more than 120,000 people who cannot tell their right hand from their _____ and also _____ animals?" (4:9-11)

Crossword 31 – Jonah

Use these words:
anger, angry, animals, captain, cargo, forty, glad, Joppa, love, lower, Nineveh, prayed, right, sackcloth, sacrifice, sailors, second, sleeping, storm, swallow, thousand, throw, vomit, worm

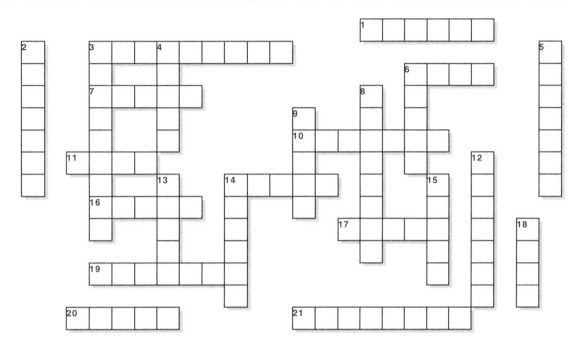

ACROSS

1 - From inside the fish, Jonah ___ to God.
3 - After the storm stopped, the sailors made a ___ to the Lord.
6 - The Lord is abounding in ___.
7 - The sailors threw away the ___ in an effort to save the ship.
10 - God told Jonah to go and preach in ___.
11 - Jonah was ___ to have shelter from the heat of the sun.
14 - The Lord sent a violent ___ on the ship.
16 - Jonah told the men to ___ him into the sea.
17 - The Lord is slow to ___.
19 - The ___ found Jonah and told him to pray.
20 - Jonah went to the seaport city of ___ and found a ship going to Tarshish.
21 - There were a hundred and twenty ___ people in the city who did not know their right hand from their left.

DOWN

2 - The ___ threw Jonah overboard.
3 - The people wore ___ to show sorrow for their sins.
4 - God asked, "Is it ___ for you to be angry?"
5 - There were also many ___ in the city.
6 - Jonah went down into the ___ part of the ship.
8 - When the storm came, Jonah was ___.
9 - Jonah was ___ when God showed compassion on the city of Nineveh.
12 - God provided a huge fish to ___ Jonah.
13 - After three days, the Lord caused the fish to ___ Jonah out on the shore.
14 - The Lord spoke to Jonah a ___ time, telling him to go to Nineveh.
15 - Jonah warned that Nineveh would be destroyed in ___ days.
18 - A ___ caused the plant to wither and die.

Storyboard 31 - Jonah

A good way to learn this story is to use the **Walk Around the Room** method. Designate spots representing these seven places. At each location, find objects that help you remember the details.

1) Jonah's home
2) Joppa
3) The ship at sea
4) Nineveh
5) In the shelter
6) The Vine
7) Place of conversation with God

▶ Another good way to learn this story is to use the boxes on the next page and draw icons for each section.

Section 1 - Disobeying God

Jonah's home:
– God's command
– Jonah's reason to disobey
– What Jonah did in Joppa

The ship at sea:
– What the sailors did to survive the storm
– The sailors' conversation with Jonah
– The three things they did after that.

Section 2 - Preaching

Trip to Nineveh:
– What happened in the fish
– What Jonah did in Nineveh

Time of Repentance:
– How the people and the king responded to Jonah's preaching

Section 3 - Conversation with God

Jonah's attitude:
– Jonah's immediate response
– God's question
– Jonah's pouting

God's vine:
– What the vine did
– How God killed it
– God and Jonah talking

God's conclusion:
– God's comments about the vine
– Saving the city

Drawing Storyboard 31 – Jonah
Using the boxes below, show the storyboard in pictures, symbols, or words.

Disobeying God

Preaching

Conversation with God

Reflection - 31

- What was your favorite part of the story? Tell why.
  _____

- What did you learn about people from the story of *Jonah*?
  _____

- What did you learn about God from the story of *Jonah*?
  _____

Communication Activities
Communicate the story in your most enjoyable form of expression.

- **Art:** Select a part of this story and paint (or draw) a picture of it.
- **Storytelling:** Form a team of three people. Each tell part of the story in first-person. One is a sailor on the ship, one is a citizen of Nineveh, and one is Jonah himself. The sailor and the citizen will tell what happened during their part of the story. Jonah will tell the beginning, the ending, and what happened in between the ship and the city. Be sure to include all the emotions involved during each part.
- **Pantomime:** Act out this story silently while someone reads it aloud.
- **Scrapbook/Poster:** Find small pictures that illustrate each part of this story and display them on a poster.
- **News Report:** Write an article on this story for the ancient *Nineveh Review* newspaper.
- **Map Activity:** Draw a map showing Judah, Israel and Assyria. Add the locations of the capitals for each.
- **Research:** Study the description and history of 'sackcloth' and give examples of times it was mentioned in the Bible.
- **Group Game:** Divide into teams. Make a copy of the story page for each team. Cut the pages into individual paragraphs and mix them up (separately). Give each team a stack of the paragraphs. Spread them out on a table and see how quickly everyone can put them into the correct order.

Student has completed one or more of the communication activities.   Teacher initials _____

Banner or Bumper Sticker: Give the essence of this story in seven words or less.

_____

Tell the story: To whom did you tell the story, and what was their response?

_____
_____

Group Discussion - 31

JONAH

1. Jonah openly told the sailors that he was running from God. Why is admitting our mistakes in front of others so difficult? How is it good (or bad) for developing relationships?

2. The sailors tried everything else before doing what Jonah said to do. Name a time when you avoided working on the basic cause of your problem, even after someone clearly pointed it out to you.

3. The sailors worshiped God after the storm stopped. When have you been in awe because you saw God do something extra ordinary?

4. The king of Nineveh humbled himself. What role does leadership play in setting the tone in times of crises? Give good or bad examples of this.

5. Jonah was furious when God spared the people of Nineveh. Name a time when something good happened to a person (or organization) you didn't like. How did you react?

NOTES:

Introduction to Lesson 32

Isaiah was a prophet in the Southern Kingdom of Judah during a time when Assyria was the dominant world power. Known for their ruthless treatment of prisoners, the Assyrians conquered nation after nation with brutal efficiency.

Their strategy for control included deporting conquered peoples to other lands, effectively erasing their sense of national identity and belonging. They would then bring in other people to occupy the conquered land. This was what happened to both Syria and the Northern Kingdom of Israel. With these nations subdued, the Southern Kingdom of Judah was the only barrier left between Assyria and their ultimate goal – the conquest of Egypt.

Sennacherib, the King of Assyria, attempted to capture Jerusalem but failed. Following Isaiah's counsel, King Hezekiah negotiated an alliance with Assyria, avoiding deportation for his people, at the cost of heavy taxes. Sennacherib then shifted his focus to Egypt and successfully conquered it.

Lesson 32 ~ The King of Assyria
Isaiah 36-37

Hezekiah was one of Judah's greatest kings, known for walking faithfully with God and honoring him. During his reign, the Assyrian Empire conquered the Northern Kingdom of Israel and exiled its people. Afterward, the Assyrians turned their attention south and invaded the Southern Kingdom, Judah.

The Assyrian commander arranged a meeting outside the walls of Jerusalem, and Hezekiah sent some of his palace officers out to represent him. The commander delivered a message from Sennacherib, the king of Assyria:

"Why are you so confident against my mighty army? No other nation will come to your aid — they all fear us." Then, mocking their faith, he added, "Oh, are you trusting in the Lord your God? Well, let me tell you this: it was your God who sent us here to destroy you!"

The Jewish delegation realized the commander was speaking loud enough so the people on the city wall could hear. They said, "Please, speak in your own language. We understand it."

The commander laughed and spoke louder, "No! This message is not only for your king. It is also for the common men who are on the wall. They are the ones who will suffer the most when we crush you."

He pointed to the men on the wall. "Listen to me! Don't trust your king or your God! Trust Sennacherib, the great king of Assyria! He will take good care of you. We have conquered many nations, and their gods were not able to protect them. Your God cannot stop the great king of Assyria!"

The delegation went back to Hezekiah and ripped their clothes in sorrow. When the king heard their report, he ripped his clothes as well. He went into the house of the Lord to pray, and sent messengers to the prophet Isaiah asking him to pray for God's people.

Isaiah sent word to Hezekiah. "The Lord says, 'I have heard this man's blaspheming! Do not be afraid. I will put a rumor into his ear and he will return to his own country. There, someone will murder him.'"

Suddenly, the commander heard of trouble in his land, and he knew the king of Assyria would need him. The entire army pulled up camp and returned to Nineveh, their capital city.

The nation of Judah was at peace for a time, until once again Sennacherib decided to move against Jerusalem. He sent a message to Hezekiah. "Did your God tell you that you were safe from the king of Assyria? Don't believe him! The other nations were not protected by their gods. I have conquered them all and burnt their gods with fire."

Hezekiah took the letter to the House of the Lord. He spread it out before God and prayed. "Oh Lord, look at this letter from the king of Assyria. He is saying you are like an idol made of wood or stone. Deliver us so all the nations of the earth will know that you alone are God."

Isaiah gave Hezekiah God's answer to King Sennacherib.

"Who do you think you are? I have commanded Jerusalem to spit on you. Who do you think you are mocking? I am the Holy God of Israel. I am the one who put you in power so you would judge other nations.

Now you have become so arrogant that you rage against me. Therefore, I am going to put a hook in your nose, put a bit in your mouth, and take you back to the barn from which you came!"

"Hezekiah, don't worry about Sennacherib. Not one arrow will hit the walls of Jerusalem. Before his armies get here, they will turn around and go back to their country. I am your defense! I will save the city because of my promises to David."

That evening the army of Assyria camped for the night. The sun went down and men sat around the campfire until it was time to sleep. When the sun arose the next morning, 185,000 solders were dead where they had slept. The great king of Assyria had an army of corpses!

He quickly returned home to Nineveh and knelt down before his idol. Two of his sons came in and killed him with a sword. Sennacherib, the great king of Assyria was dead, and Jerusalem was at peace.

Search the Scriptures 32 - The King of Assyria
Isaiah 36-37

1. While _____ was king of Judah, Sennacherib, the king of _____ invaded Judah. He sent his commander with a huge army to the city of _____. (36:1-2)

2. Some of King Hezekiah's palace officers came outside the _____ to meet with the Assyrian army _____. He gave them a message from his king to their king: "In whom are you trusting? If you are trusting in Pharaoh, king of _____, he will be no help you. If you are trusting in your God, he is the one who sent me to _____ your land." (36:3-10)

3. Hezekiah's officers replied, "Speak to us in the Aramaic _____, because we understand it; don't speak in Hebrew within the hearing of the men on the _____."

4. The commander spoke _____, "These words are for the _____ on the wall. They are the ones who will suffer the most when we conquer you." (36:12-13)

5. "Don't believe Hezekiah when he says, 'The Lord will _____ us.'" (36:15)

6. The palace officers _____ their clothes and went back to King Hezekiah and told him the _____ of the Assyrian army commander. (36:22)

7. When King Hezekiah heard this he tore his _____, covered himself with sackcloth, and went into the _____ of the Lord. (37:1)

8. Hezekiah sent messengers to the prophet Isaiah and asked him to _____ for the Lord's people. (37:2-4)

9. The prophet Isaiah told the messengers to tell King Hezekiah, "Do not be _____. The army commander will hear a rumor and _____ to his own land and fall by the _____ in his own land." Soon, the _____ returned to his own country. (37:5-8)

10. Then the _____ of Assyria sent messengers with a letter for King Hezekiah. When he received it, he took it to the House of the Lord and _____ it out before the Lord. (37:14)

11. Hezekiah wanted God to _____ and _____ all the words of Sennacherib that he sent to mock the _____ God. (37:17)

12. The king of Assyria had destroyed many other nations, and he _____ their gods that were made of _____ and stone. Hezekiah prayed, "Oh, Lord, our God, _____ us from his hand so that _____ the kingdoms of the earth will _____ that you alone are the Lord." (37:19-20)

13. Then the prophet Isaiah sent a message: "This is what the _____ has spoken <u>to</u> Sennacherib, king of Assyria . . . 'Because you have raged against me . . . I will put my _____ in your nose and my _____ in your mouth, and I will make you return on the way by which you came.'" (37:29)

14. This is what the Lord says <u>concerning</u> the king of Assyria: "He shall not come into this _____ or shoot an _____ there. I will _____ this city to save it for my own _____ and for the sake of my servant _____." (37:33-35)

15. The angel of the Lord went to the _____ of the Assyrians and struck down _____ men.

16. Sennacherib returned home to _____ where two of his sons came and _____ him. (37:37-38)

Crossword 32 – The King of Assyria

Use these words:
afraid, arrow, clothes, commander, God, Hezekiah, hook, Isaiah, letter, living, Nineveh, returned, rumor, sackcloth, Sennacherib, sons, spread, tore, wall, wood

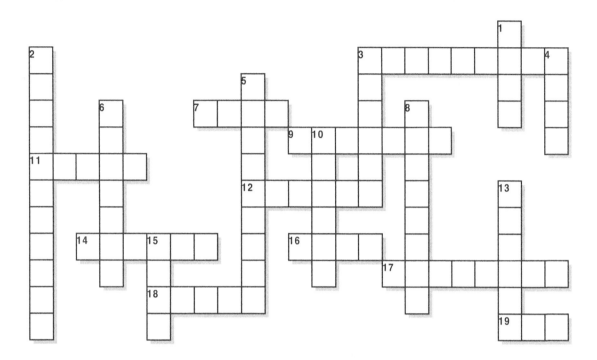

ACROSS

3 - King Hezekiah covered himself in ___ and went into the House of the Lord.

7 - The Assyrians destroyed many nations and burned their gods made of ___ and stone.

9 - Sennacherib's home was in ___.

11 - God said the king of Assyria would not come into Jerusalem or shoot an ___ there.

12 - God's message to Hezekiah: "Do not be ___."

14 - KIng Hezekiah received a ___ from King Sennacherib.

16 - The army commander wanted the men on the ___ to hear him.

17 - ___ was the king of Judah

18 - "The army commander will hear a ___ and return to his own country."

19 - The Assyrians claimed they had been sent by ___ to destroy Jerusalem. (Isa 36:10)

DOWN

1 - Sennacherib's ___ killed him.

2 - The king of Assyria was named ___.

3 - Hezekiah went to the Temple and ___ out the letter from Sennacherib.

4 - God's words to the king of Assyria: "I will put my ___ in your nose and my bit in your mouth . . ."

5 - The ___ of the Assyrian army met with King Hezekiah's palace officers outside the wall of Jerusalem.

6 - King Hezekiah tore his ___.

8 - The commander heard of trouble in his own land, and he ___ home.

10 - The prophet ___ encouraged Hezekiah.

13 - Sennacherib's words were an insult to the ___ God

15 - Hezekiah's palace officers ___ their clothes.

Storyboard 32 – The King of Assyria

Section 1 – Threats at the Wall

This is a conversation between the Assyrian commander and the delegation of Judah. The best way to remember it is through hand gestures.

☛ Create your own hand movements that will help you tell what was said and what happened.

Section 2 – Reaction to the Threats

This second section tells about the king reacting to the commander.
Remember these words:

                RIP, RIP — PRAYER — MESSAGE — EAR, EAR — MURDER

Here is the meaning:

    RIP, RIP (delegation and king)
        — pretend to rip your clothes twice
    PRAYER
        — hands together in prayer
    MESSAGE
        — give a message off to the side
    EAR, EAR
        — **hand behind one ear** *I have heard*
        — **hand behind the other ear** *I will put a rumor into his ear*
    MURDER
        — **hand motion indicating murder** *Someone will murder him*

Section 3 – Threats by Letter

☛ Create hand gestures **OR** ▶ Draw icons to remember the words of these two kings.

    Sennacherib's letter <u>about</u> God
        God lied
        Other nations
    Hezekiah's comments <u>to</u> God
        Look at his letter
        It says you are like idols
        Deliver us

Section 4 – God's Message to the King of Assyria

☛ Build this part of the story around the following hand gestures:

    point out — *Who do you think you are?*

    point in — *Who do you think you're mocking?*

    make your finger into a hook — *I am going to put a hook in your nose…*

    point to Hezekiah — *Don't worry about…*

    both hands out and open — *army of Assyria camped*

    point off in the distance — *quickly returned home*

Drawing Storyboard 32 – The King of Assyria

Using the boxes below, show the storyboard in pictures, symbols, or words.

Threats at the Wall	Reaction to the Threats
Threats by Letter	God's Message to the King of Assyria

Reflection – 32

- What was your favorite part of the story? Tell why.
  _____

- What did you learn about people from *The King of Assyria?*
  _____

- What did you learn about God from *The King of Assyria?*
  _____

Communication Activities
Communicate the story in your most enjoyable form of expression.

- **Art:** Select a part of this story and paint (or draw) a picture of it.
- **Dramatic Monologue:** Have two people tell this story as if they are Hezekiah and his wife telling it to their grandchildren.
- **Music:** Write a ballad that tells this story in song. Do it as if it is written by a resident of ancient Jerusalem, who is rejoicing after their victory over Assyria.
- **Poetry:** Practice and Perform the famous poem. *The Destruction of Sennacherib* by Lord Byron first published in 1815. It is based on an event described in the Bible during the campaign by King Sennacherib to capture Jerusalem.
- **News Report:** Write an article about this victory as if it is for the ancient *Jerusalem Times*.
- **On-Site Reporter:** Pose as a reporter who has come to interview people about their victory over the Assyrians. The reporter had been away on another assignment so doesn't know the details of what happened. Those being interviewed could be common citizens, Hezekiah, Isaiah, some of the people on the wall, and an Assyrian slave who escaped.
- **Pantomime:** Act out this story silently while someone reads it aloud.

Student has completed one or more of the communication activities.   Teacher initials _____

Banner or Bumper Sticker: Give the essence of this story in seven words or less.

┌──┐
│   │
└──┘

Tell the story: To whom did you tell the story, and what was their response?
_____
_____

Group Discussion - 32

THE KING OF ASSYRIA

1. The Assyrian commander mocked the Jews' faith in God. How do you respond when others make fun of your faith?

2. Hezekiah and his palace officers tore their clothes to express their sorrow. In our society, how do we express grief or distress. How does it help us deal with difficult emotions?

3. When faced with King Sennacherib's threat, Hezekiah went to the temple and prayed. How do you express your trust in God when faced with worries and fears?

4. King Hezekiah sought Isaiah's counsel during the crisis. Who do you have who gives you wise advice in difficult situations? How can we discern who we should trust?

5. The Assyrian army had an overwhelming force, yet they failed. Tell of a time when you felt overwhelmed, but remained steadfast in your faith? How did it turn out?

NOTES:

Introduction to Lesson 33

Jeremiah was born into a priestly family in Judah. He gave prophecies about the destruction of Jerusalem and about the Southern Kingdom of Judah's exile in Babylon.

His prophecies foretold their exile but also offered hope for the future and the eventual restoration of Israel with the rebuilding of Jerusalem.

Jeremiah faced major persecution from the people and rulers of Judah due to his harsh messages. He was imprisoned, beaten, and threatened with death. He has become known as the "Weeping Prophet."

His prophecies have meaning today because they talk about a new covenant that God will make with his people — a covenant based on internal transformation rather than external laws.

Lesson 33 – Jeremiah
Jeremiah 1-36   II Chronicles 36   II Kings 24-25

God called Jeremiah to preach to the people of Judah. "Lord, I don't want this job."

The Lord made his calling clear. "I chose you for this job before you were born. I'll tell you exactly what to say."

He then sent Jeremiah to the potter's house. The prophet saw the potter working with a clay jar on the turning wheel. Suddenly the potter found a flaw in the jar. He simply crushed it and started over. The Lord said to Jeremiah, "Give this message to Israel. You're like clay in my hands and I'm about to crush you so I can make you into that which has my blessing and joy."

Jeremiah took a clay jar and stood before the rulers of Judah. He held it in the air and said, "The people have forsaken the Lord to worship idols." Then the prophet threw the jar down, and it shattered into pieces. "Hear what the Lord says: 'Like this clay jar, I'll destroy Jerusalem. The people will be slaughtered, and the city will lie in ruins!'"

A certain priest had Jeremiah beaten and put in stocks. The next day Jeremiah told him, "The Lord has changed your name to 'Terror.' In terror, you'll see your friends killed in the streets. In terror, you'll watch the city be destroyed. You'll be taken to Babylon where you'll die; and there you'll be buried."

Jeremiah preached boldly at the Temple, warning the people that God was going to destroy it because of their evil ways. After that, the prophet was banned from going back to the Temple.

The Lord told Jeremiah, "Write a book of all the things I've told you about the coming judgment on Judah and Jerusalem." So, Jeremiah dictated to his scribe everything the Lord said. When they were done, the scribe was told to go to the Temple and read it to the people.

While the scribe was there reading the book, government officials listened. They said, "The king needs to hear this!" They got permission to take the book and read it in the palace.

The king was sitting in front of a fire because it was winter. Every time a portion of the book was read, he cut that part out and threw it into the fire, until it was totally destroyed.

The Lord said to Jeremiah, "Write another book, just like the one that was burned. Also, give this message to the king. 'Your dead body won't be buried but will rot in the open sun. Furthermore, your descendants will not inherit the throne of David.'"

Jeremiah told the people of Judah, "Babylon will come and destroy this city and take you into captivity. You'll be there for seventy years. After that, God will bring your children back to this land."

It happened just like the prophet said. The king of Babylon invaded Judah and conquered it. But the people there kept rebelling, so the army of Babylon had to conduct three separate invasions. Each was more devastating than the one before.

The first time, they took everything out of the Temple to be used in the heathen temples of their gods. They took the king captive and the best of the young people.

The second time, they removed more treasures from the House of the Lord and the king's palace. They took more than ten thousand captives, including officers, soldiers, craftsmen, and artisans. They left behind the poorest people so they could tend the land.

The third time, they burned the House of the Lord, and all the houses of Jerusalem. They also broke down the walls around Jerusalem.

God gave Jeremiah a vision. The Lord said, "What do you see?"

"I see two baskets of figs. One is full of the most delicious looking fruit I've ever seen. The other has rotten figs that smell awful."

God said, "The people here in Judah are like rotten figs — corrupt and spoiled beyond use. I'll send them heartache, plague, and famine. By the time I'm finished, they'll be cast aside like garbage.

But the people who've been taken to Babylon are like the good figs. They can call on me anytime, and I'll listen. When their exile ends, I'll bring them back and restore what they left behind. I'll watch over them and care for them. Their children will return to this land, and their hearts will be drawn to know me. I will be their God, and they will be my people."

Search the Scriptures 33 ~ Jeremiah
Jeremiah 1-36   II Chronicles 36   II Kings 24-25

1. The Lord said to Jeremiah, "I have put my _____ in your mouth." (Jer. 1:9)

2. God said, "Go to the _____ house and I will speak to you. "Oh, house of Israel . . . as the clay in the potter's _____, so are _____ in my hand." (Jer. 18:1-6)

3. The _____ told Jeremiah to take a clay jar and go tell the people and priests, "Because you have forsaken me to worship _____ gods, I am going to destroy Jerusalem." (Jer. 19:1-7)

4. Then Jeremiah was to _____ the clay jar, and tell the people, "I will destroy this nation and city just as the potter's jar is _____ and cannot be repaired." (Jer. 19:10-11)

5. When the priest heard this, he had Jeremiah _____ and put in stocks. The next day, Jeremiah said to the _____, "The Lord has changed your name to '_____.' In terror, you'll see your friends _____ in the streets. You will be taken to _____ where you will die." (Jer. 20:1-6)

6. God told Jeremiah to stand at the gate of the _____ and warn the people to change their ways or he would destroy the Temple and the city of _____. (Jer. 7:3, 30-34)

7. Babylon's army invaded Judah and Jerusalem _____ times. Each time, they took the king captive and carried away treasures from the _____. They took thousands of captives, including the best of the young _____, leaving only the _____ people to tend the land. (II Kings 24)

8. On their last invasion, they _____ the House of the Lord, the king's house, and all the houses of Jerusalem. They also broke down the _____ around Jerusalem and burned them. (II Kings 25:1-10)

9. The Lord appeared to Jeremiah in a vision. He showed him two baskets of _____ sitting in front of the Temple. One basket had very _____ figs, and the other basket had very _____ figs. (Jer. 24:1-3)

10. God said the good figs were like the people taken away _____ to a foreign land; He would keep his _____ on them and bring them back to their _____ and plant them there. (Jer. 24:5-6)

11. God said, "They shall be my _____, and I will be their _____, for they shall _____ to me with their whole heart." The bad _____ symbolized those people who remained with the evil King Zedekiah in the land but were later carried away and destroyed. (Jer. 24:7-10)

12. God said, "Because you have _____ listened to me or obeyed me . . . I will _____ your nation, and you will serve the king of Babylon for _____ years." (Jer. 25:8-11)

13. The Lord said, "After seventy _____ in captivity, I will visit you and fulfill my promise and _____ you back to your own land. I know the _____ I have for you — plans for good and not evil — plans to give you a _____ and a hope. (Jer. 29:10-11)

14. You will seek me and _____ me when you search for me with all your _____. (Jer. 29:13)

15. I will be _____ by you, and I will restore your fortunes and gather you . . . and bring you back to the places from which I sent you into _____." (Jer. 29:14)

16. When Jeremiah's book was read to the king, he _____ it in the fire. After that, God commanded Jeremiah to write _____ book exactly like the first. (Jer. 36: 21-30)

Crossword 33 – Jeremiah

Use these words:
another, baskets, beaten, born, break, burned, destroyed, exile, eyes, hand, heart know, land, other, seventy, terror, three, treasures, walls, words

ACROSS

1 - God promised to bring his people back to their own ___ after their exile in Babylon.
7 - The captivity was to last for ___ years.
9 - God said to Jeremiah, "I have put my ___ in your mouth."
10 - You will seek me and find me when you search for me with all your ___.
11 - The good figs symbolized the people who were in ___.
12 - The king of Babylon conducted ___ separate invasions of Judah.
13 - The Lord showed Jeremiah two ___ of figs.
15 - The Babylonian army carried away all the ___ from the House of the Lord.
16 - God said he would give the captives a desire to ___ him. (Jer. 24:7)
17 - God's people turned away from him to serve ___ gods.
18 - "As the clay in the potter's hand, so are you in my ___."

DOWN

2 - After Jeremiah's book was burned, God told him to write ___ one exactly like it.
3 - A priest had Jeremiah ___ and put in stocks.
4 - Jeremiah was instructed to ___ the clay jar in front of the people and priests.
5 - God chose Jeremiah to be a prophet before he was ___.
6 - God warned his people that their nation and city would be ___ if they turned away from him.
8 - God said he would keep his ___ on the people who were in exile.
9 - The Babylonian army broke down the ___ of Jerusalem.
13 - The Babylonian army ___ the Temple, the king's palace, and all the houses in Jerusalem.
14 - Jeremiah told the priest his new name would be '___.'

Storyboard 33 - Jeremiah

Section 1 - A Broken Jar

▶ Remember the sequence of this section by putting four drawings together, similar to a comic strip, in the first box on the next page.

- Panel 1 – God's call
- Panel 2 – Learning from the potter
- Panel 3 – Breaking the jar
- Panel 4 – A man named 'Terror'

☛ You may choose to develop hand gestures that represent the parts of Section 1.

Section 2 - Burning the Book

▶ Remember the sequence of this section by putting five drawings together, like a comic strip, in the second box on the next page.

- Panel 1 – Jeremiah preaching in the Temple
- Panel 2 – Jeremiah writing the book
- Panel 3 – His scribe reading aloud and government officials listening
- Panel 4 – The king burning the book
- Panel 5 – Jeremiah rewriting the book with a message of doom for the king

Section 3 - The Destruction of Jerusalem

▶ In the third box on the next page, draw icons to show what Babylon's army did during the three times they invaded Judah and Jerusalem.

1) Jeremiah's famous prophesy about the seventy years of captivity
2) What Babylon's army did/took when they invaded Judah

Section 4 - Two Baskets of Figs

This section is Jeremiah's prophecy about two baskets of figs which illustrate the future of Israel during their time of captivity. The story provides its own storyboard, but it's important to remember God's promises for those in captivity:

1. I am going to watch over my people and care for them.
2. I will bring their descendants back into this land and once again plant them here.
3. I will put a desire in their hearts to know me.
4. I will be their God and they shall be my people.

❖ Use your favorite way to learn this list — drawings, hand gestures, or walk around the room.

Drawing Storyboard 33 – Jeremiah

Using the boxes below, show the storyboard in pictures, symbols, or words.

A Broken Jar	*Burning the Book*
The Destruction of Jerusalem	*Two Baskets of Figs*

Reflection – 33

- What was your favorite part of the story? Tell why.
  _____

- What did you learn about people from the story of *Jeremiah*?
  _____

- What did you learn about God from the story of *Jeremiah*?
  _____

Communication Activities
Communicate the story in your most enjoyable form of expression.

- **Art:** Select a part of this story and paint (or draw) a picture of it.
- **Storytelling:** Form a team of four people. Each tell a section of the story in first-person. One will be the potter after he heard what the prophet did with his pot. Jeremiah's scribe telling what happened to the book. One of the few people left in Judah after the third invasion. One of the people in captivity reading Jeremiah's "Two Basket of Figs" prophecy. Be sure to include all the emotions involved during each part.
- **Music:** Write a ballad that tells this story in song. Have four verses for the four sections.
- **Poetry:** Write a poem that retells this story.
- **Research:** Study *Leviticus 25:1-7, 26:14-35,* and *II Chronicles 36:20-21.* Tell why the Lord's people were removed from their land and had to stay in exile for seventy years.
- **News Report:** Write an article as if from a reporter for a newspaper in Babylon. The people there have heard about the famous prophet in Judah and want to know more about him.
- **Map Activity:** Draw a map showing Judah and Babylon. Add the locations of the capitals for each.

Student has completed one or more of the communication activities.   Teacher initials _____

Banner or Bumper Sticker: Give the essence of this story in seven words or less.

[   ]

Tell the story: To whom did you tell the story, and what was their response?
_____
_____

Group Discussion - 33

Jeremiah

1. At first, Jeremiah resisted God's calling. When have you felt unqualified (or unwilling) to take on God's challenge?

2. The potter's wheel was used to show how God is shaping his people. When have you felt like God was reshaping you?

3. The potter crushed the jar and remade it, which illustrates how God deals with us. Tell of a time when you have been broken down and became something better.

4. A priest had Jeremiah beaten for speaking the truth. Give an illustration of people resisting truth, only to have things get worse.

5. Jeremiah told the people that their exile was temporary, and restoration would come. Have you helped someone see past their current struggles and envision a brighter future?

6. Read the prophet's message to the exiles in Babylon (*Jeremiah 29:4-7*). How can we apply this to our lives today?

NOTES:

Introduction to Lesson 34

The people of Judah were exiles in Babylon during the time when it was conquered by Cyrus the Great of Persia. During the 70 years of captivity, Daniel served in the royal courts for both kingdoms.

The first of the two events in this lesson happened at the beginning of the 70 years. The second event happened near the end of that time.

God had told Jeremiah how long the people would be in captivity. God told Daniel what would happen after their captivity was over.

Daniel's prophecies go far into the future including the coming of Christ. Some of them go to the end of time.

Lesson 34 ~ Daniel
Daniel 1 & 6

Nebuchadnezzar was king of Babylon. He had conquered Jerusalem and taken many people captive. He ordered his officials to select the best young men and train them to serve in the royal court. This training would last three years and included instruction in the language and literature of Babylon. During that time, the king would provide them the finest food and wine.

Four of the young men selected were Daniel, Shadrach, Meshach, and Abednego. These men determined not to defile themselves by eating and drinking things that went against God's Law. Daniel asked their overseer to leave those things out of their daily diet.

"Oh no. I can't do that! A day is coming when you'll stand before the king. He'll have me killed when he sees that you are scrawnier than the others!"

Daniel chose his words carefully. "Before you decide, please do a test. Allow the four of us to eat vegetables and drink water for ten days. Then see how we look in comparison to the others."

The overseer agreed to this idea because he highly respected Daniel. At the end of ten days, Daniel and his friends looked better and healthier than all the others. So, the overseer allowed the four of them to continue eating only vegetables and drinking water.

God was with Daniel and his friends, giving them knowledge, wisdom, and understanding. At the end of three years, they ranked higher than all the others, so they began serving in the king's court.

Daniel continued to serve in the court through the reign of many kings. When he was an older man, there was a new king who appointed three high officials to assist him. One of these was Daniel and he was the most capable of all. King Darius was about to give him authority over the entire kingdom.

The other officials were jealous and searched for a way to make Daniel look bad to the king. They tried to find some kind of corruption in what he did for the government, but there was nothing. Finally, they said, "There's only one way we can do this. We must find something having to do with the laws of his God."

They went to the king and said, "Oh, King, live forever! We have thought of a way to honor you. Please create a law that says no one can pray to any god except you for 30 days. Anyone who disobeys this law will be thrown into the den of lions." The king liked the idea, so he signed the decree.

Despite hearing about the new law, Daniel continued praying three times a day. He went into his room, opened the windows facing Jerusalem, knelt down, and prayed to God.

Immediately, the other men went to the king. "Didn't you sign a decree that says no one can pray to any god except you, or they will be thrown into a den of lions?"

"Yes, I did. I made it a special law that can't be changed."

"Oh, king, it makes us sad to tell you that Daniel is breaking that law. He prays and worships his God three times a day."

The king knew instantly that he had made a terrible mistake! He wanted to protect Daniel, so he worked diligently to find a way to change the law; but it couldn't be done.

With a heavy heart, he gave the order to put Daniel into the lions' den. A huge stone with the king's seal was placed over the opening so that no one could stop the punishment. The king was miserable! He went to his palace and canceled all his plans for the evening. He didn't eat or sleep all night.

In the morning, he rushed to the lions' den and ordered the stone removed. The king yelled, "Daniel, servant of the Most High God, was your God able to save you from the lions?"

Daniel called back to him, "Oh, King, live forever! My God sent his angel to shut the mouths of the lions. I have not been hurt in any way." With joy, the king gave the order to have Daniel brought up out of the lions' den.

The king then turned and said to his guards, "Go get those men who came up with this idea against Daniel and throw them into the den of lions."

It was done exactly as the king commanded. The lions were waiting at the bottom of the pit. They ripped those men apart before they reached the floor!

King Darius wrote a new law and sent it out to people of all languages in his kingdom. It said, "Everyone is to fear Daniel's God because he is the living God. His kingdom will last forever, and he is able to save those who serve him."

Search the Scriptures 34 - Daniel
Daniel 1 & 6

1. When Nebuchadnezzar's army invaded Jerusalem, they captured many young men from the royal family. These were taken into the king's court and given _____ and wine from the king's table. They were educated in language and literature for _____ years and then appear before the king. Among these was Daniel. (1:4-6)

2. Daniel and his friends _____ that they would not defile themselves with the king's food. Daniel asked the overseer for _____ not to eat those things. The overseer said, "I am afraid that the king might see you in _____ condition than the others, and I would be in trouble." (1:8-10)

3. Then Daniel said to him, "Test us for _____ days, and let us be given _____ to eat and _____ to drink. Then see how we look, and deal with us according to what you see." (1:12-13)

4. So he agreed to the idea and tested them for ten days. At the end of ten days they looked _____ healthy than all the others who ate the king's food. At the end of three years, they were brought to Nebuchadnezzar, and he talked with them. In matters of wisdom and understanding, the king found Daniel and his friends ten times _____ than all the other 'wise men' in his kingdom. (1:14-20)

5. Years later, when _____ became king, he appointed three high officials, one of whom was Daniel. King Darius planned to put Daniel over the _____ kingdom. He was distinguished _____ all the others because he had an excellent spirit. (6:1-3)

6. The other officials tried to find _____ with Daniel, but there wasn't any valid complaint, because he did everything _____. They said, "We won't find anything against him unless it has something to do with the law of his _____." (6:4-5)

7. So they went to the king and said, "O King, live _____! We all agree you should make a law that if anyone _____ to any god or human except you, he will be thrown into the lions' _____. So, King Darius made the law. When _____ heard about it, he went to his _____, got down on his _____ three times a day and prayed to God, just as he had done before. (6:7-10)

8. The other men _____ him praying and then _____ to the king. "O king, did you not sign a decree that anyone who prays to any god or man except to _____ would be thrown into the lions' den?" The king answered, "_____, it is a law that cannot be _____." (6:11-12)

9. They said, "Daniel, one of the exiles from _____ pays no attention to you or to your law. He prays _____ times a day." The king was greatly _____ and he was determined to find a way to _____ Daniel. But the law couldn't be changed. (6:13-15)

10. So, the king gave the order and they brought Daniel and _____ him into the lions' den. The king spoke to Daniel, "May your God, whom you _____ continually, deliver you!" Then he went to his palace and spent the night. He did not _____ and he couldn't _____. (6:16-18)

11. At daybreak, he got up and _____ to the lions' den. He cried out in a tone of anguish, "O Daniel, servant of the _____ God, has your God whom you serve continually been able to _____ you from the lions?" (6:19-20)

12. Daniel answered, "O King, live forever! My God sent his angel and _____ the lions' mouths, and they have not _____ me." The king was exceedingly _____, and commanded that Daniel be lifted up out of the den. The men who had gotten Daniel in trouble were immediately thrown into the lions' den. (6:21-24)

13. King Darius wrote a new law: "In my kingdom, people must _____ the God of Daniel, for he is the living _____, enduring forever. His kingdom shall never be destroyed . . . He has _____ Daniel from the power of the lions." (6:25-27)

Crossword 34 - Daniel

Use these words:

afraid, better, court, Daniel, defile, distressed, fault, forever, glad, jealous, Jerusalem, language law, living, men, pray, save, servant, shut, ten, test, three, thrown, vegetables

ACROSS

2 - When Daniel served King Darius, the other court officials were ___ of him.

5 - The king was exceedingly ___ when he saw that Daniel was not harmed by the lions.

9 - When the army of Babylon invaded Jerusalem, they took ___ captive.

11 - King Darius made a law that people could not ___ to anyone except him for 30 days.

12 - Daniel said God sent an angel to ___ the mouths of the lions.

15 - The men who had made trouble for Daniel were themselves ___ into the den of lions.

16 - Daniel did not want to ___ himself by eating the king's food.

18 - Daniel proposed a ___ to compare diets.

19 - The young ___ in the court were expected to eat the king's food and drink his wine.

22 - Daniel and his friends wanted to eat just ___ and water for ten days.

23 - Daniel and his friends were in a ___ - year training program.

24 - Daniel served in the ___ through the reign of many kings.

DOWN

1 - Daniel knelt and prayed in his room by a window facing ___.

3 - The young men taken to Babylon were taught the ___ and literature of that city.

4 - Some things Daniel was expected to eat went against God's ___.

6 - The overseer was ___ that the young men might not look as healthy as they should.

7 - The king called Daniel a ___ of the living God.

8 - King Darius was greatly ___ when he realized his law could bring harm to Daniel.

10 - King Darius made a new law that said everyone was to worship the ___ God.

13 - After three years, the king found Daniel and his friends ten times ___ than all the other wise men.

14 - The people's greeting was, "O, King, live ___!"

17 - The king's officials could not find any ___ in Daniel.

20 - After ___ days, Daniel and his friends looked better than all the others.

21 - King Darius said that Daniel's God was able to ___ those who serve him.

Storyboard 34 - Daniel

Section 1 - Food and Wine

This first section is a simple narrative. Make a few drawings on the facing page to help you remember the order of events.

There are a couple of small lists that can be remembered by using fingers on both hands.

- Three fingers on left hand — training for three years
- Three fingers on right hand — language, literature, and wisdom (LLW)
- The three fingers on the left hand become four
  (Daniel, Shadrach, Meshach, and Abednego)

Section 2 - Three Times a Day

This second section divides into four parts. Draw reminders in the second box on the facing page.
- What King Darius was about to do
- Jealousy of the other officials
- Their scheme to get rid of Daniel
- Daniel's continued habits.

Section 3 - Den of Lions

This section divides into five parts. Draw reminders in the third box on the facing page.
- The officials tricking the king
- The king forced to put Daniel in the den
- The next morning
- What happened to the officials
- The new law

Additional Learning Technique

Because this story includes so many locations, **walk around the room** would be a good way to learn the series of events.
- Babylon
- Jerusalem
- Royal court of Nebuchadnezzar
- Where the young men stayed
- Royal court of Darius
- Place where the officials agreed on a plan
- Daniel's room
- Lions' den

Drawing Storyboard 34 – Daniel
Using the boxes below, show the storyboard in pictures, symbols, or words.

Food and Wine

Three Times a Day

Den of Lions

Reflection ~ 34

- What was your favorite part of the story? Tell why.
  _____

- What did you learn about people from the story of *Daniel?*
  _____

- What did you learn about God from the story of *Daniel?*
  _____

Communication Activities
Communicate the story in your most enjoyable form of expression.

- **Map Activity:** Draw a map showing the location of the empires of Babylon and Persia. Include the location of Jerusalem.

- **Drama:** Write a drama for one of these two events in Daniel's life.

- **Music:** Write a ballad about Daniel's experiences.

- **Research:** Study and report on the meaning of the prophecy found in *Daniel 2.*

- **Research:** Study and report on the meaning of the prophecy found in *Daniel 9:20-27.*

- **Storytelling:**
    - Create a series of "mini-stories" from the perspectives of different characters.
    - Tell the story using different hats for the various characters.
    - Tell the story using at least five different objects to illustrate it.

- **Interview:** Enlist several volunteers to be on a Biblical panel. Once they sit in a panelist chair, they are to stay 'in character.' The panel would include, Daniel, the overseer, King Nebuchadnezzar, King Darius, friends of the government officials who died in the Lions' Den, and the person in charge of the Lions' Den. Ask several questions to each person on the panel, then allow your audience to ask them questions.

Student has completed one or more of the communication activities. Teacher initials _____

Banner or Bumper Sticker: Give the essence of this story in seven words or less.

Tell the story: To whom did you tell the story, and what was their response?
_____
_____

Group Discussion - 34

Daniel

1. Daniel and his friends remained faithful to God's law. Name a situation in today's world where Believers have to go against the laws of the land or the rules of the organization.

2. The overseer resisted Daniel's request for a different diet. Yet, Daniel was determined not to go against God's commands. Still, he was careful to treat the overseer with respect. How can we do that in today's culture?

3. Daniel's consistent integrity allowed him to serve through the reign of many kings. How has your integrity impacted your relationships, careers, and spiritual journey?

4. God gave Daniel a calmness when he faced the lions. Share a time when God gave you a sense of calm in the face of danger.

5. Daniel remained faithful in his daily prayers despite the risks. How has your regular spiritual devotion sustained you during times of crisis?

Notes:

Introduction to Lesson 35

This story describes the Jewish people's journey from exile to restoration. It tells about their return from Babylon and their success in rebuilding the Temple and the walls of Jerusalem. God used many people to help them reach their goals.

- The Persian king, Cyrus, gave them permission to rebuild the temple and provided supplies and money to make it happen.

- The prophet Haggai encouraged them to prioritize the rebuilding of the Lord's House and promised God's blessing and protection.

- Ezra, a Jewish scribe and priest went to Jerusalem to make sure the Temple was constructed according to divine instructions.

- Nehemiah was a Jewish official in the Persian king's court. He was appointed governor over the land of Judah to organize the rebuilding of the city walls.

Lesson 35 ~ Returning to Jerusalem
Ezra 1-6, Haggai 1-2, Nehemiah 1-11

The prophecy of Jeremiah said that the people of Judah would be in captivity for 70 years. At the end of that time, the king of Persia made a proclamation that the Jews living in his kingdom were free to go back to Jerusalem and rebuild their temple. Their neighbors were to give silver, gold, and supplies to those who were going back.

The king also ordered his officials to return all the things Babylon's army had taken from the Temple in Jerusalem. The royal treasurer carefully counted thousands of precious items, including knives, gold and silver platters, gold and silver basins, and other treasures. All these were sent back to Jerusalem.

The king paid masons and carpenters. He also purchased cedar logs from Lebanon and transported them to the port of Joppa.

Soon after the people arrived in Judah, the non-Jewish people living there started making trouble for them. When there was a new king in Persia, the troublemakers wrote a letter to him saying the Jews were rebuilding a "rebellious city." When the king read the letter, he sent officers who forced the work to stop.

The people of Judah were disappointed, but this gave them a chance to build their own houses. One family after another started taking some of the cedar from the building site until it was all gone. Whenever someone suggested rebuilding the Temple, the people said, "This isn't a good time to build." They knew they couldn't do it without the cedar from Lebanon.

God sent the prophet Haggai with this message: "Consider your ways! You live in cedar-paneled houses while my house lies in ruins. Go into the hills and get common wood and use that in the temple. I will be pleased with what you build, and I will be glorified." The people obeyed and went into the hills and got wood to replace the missing cedar. Then they restarted the project.

God sent another message. "The glory of this temple will be greater than you can imagine. The 'Desire of all Nations' will come, and I'll fill this temple with glory. Be strong and keep your eyes focused on the present work. I'm with you as I've always been."

The troublemakers once again tried to stop them. The Jews appealed to yet another new king, a man named Darius. He searched the archives and found the decree from King Cyrus, which said, "Let the temple be rebuilt." So King Darius wrote a letter saying, "No one is to interfere with rebuilding the temple of God on its site." The Jews continued to build and prosper. In four years' time, they finished the temple. Still, Jerusalem didn't have walls to protect the city.

Nehemiah was a Jewish man who served in the court of the king of Persia. Visitors from Judah came and told him his people were suffering because the walls of Jerusalem were in ruins. Hearing that, he sat down and cried. He mourned and fasted for days.

The king saw he was greatly troubled and asked, "Why are you so sad?" Nehemiah told him about the situation in Jerusalem and asked if he could go and help. In response, the king appointed Nehemiah as governor of Judah and sent him there, accompanied by captains of the army and soldiers on horseback.

When he arrived, he spent three days looking over the situation. Finally, he met with the leaders and explained that the king had sent him to oversee the rebuilding of the city walls. He said, "We can't live with this disgrace any longer!" The people agreed. They decided that each leader would choose a section of the wall as his personal responsibility. They immediately organized their families to start building.

Their enemies tried to stop them. They mocked and insulted saying, "If they build a stone wall, it will be worthless and fall down even if a fox climbs on it."

The builders were determined and worked faster. Soon the wall was halfway up, and they started joining the various sections. Their enemies threatened to sneak up and kill them. Fear gripped the hearts of the builders, so they set up guards to watch day and night. Nehemiah spoke to the workers: "Don't be afraid. Remember the Lord who is great and awesome. Fight for your brothers, your sons, your daughters, your wives, and your houses!" So the builders kept their weapons with them while they worked on the wall.

It took only fifty-two days to complete the project. At last the city was protected. When their enemies and surrounding nations heard of this achievement, they were afraid because they realized the work had been done with God's help.

On a set day, the people assembled and Ezra read the law of God to them from morning until noon. They listened intently, worshiped the Lord and wept. Nehemiah said, "This day is holy to the Lord. Don't mourn or weep. Enjoy choice foods and sweet drinks, and send some to those who have none . . . Don't be grieved, for the joy of the Lord is your strength." So all the people went their way with great rejoicing.

Search the Scriptures 35 ~ Returning to Jerusalem
Ezra 1 – 6, Haggai 1 – 2, Nehemiah 1-11

1. After 70 years, _____, the king of Persia made a proclamation that any of God's people living in his kingdom were free to go back to Jerusalem to _____ their temple. The king ordered their neighbors to give silver, _____, and supplies to those who were going back. (Ezra 1:1-4)

2. The king also ordered his officials to find all the treasures that _____ had stolen from the Lord's _____ and brought to Babylon for the house of his gods.

3. The king's _____ carefully counted out thousands of items — gold and silver platters and basins, bronze censers, and much more. There were _____ items in all. (Ezra 1:7-11)

4. The king purchased _____ logs from Lebanon and transported them to _____. (Ezra 3:7)

5. Certain enemies who lived in the land wrote a _____ to the new king and claimed that the Jews were rebuilding that "_____ and evil city." When the _____ received the letter, he sent officers to _____ the workers to stop. (Ezra 4:4-24)

6. Meanwhile, the prophets _____ and Zechariah preached to the people of Judah and Jerusalem. They encouraged them to again begin _____ the temple. (Ezra 5:1-2)

7. When their enemies tried to stop them, the Jews said they had permission to build from King Cyrus and they appealed to the new king, _____, asking him to search the archives at _____ for proof. He did so and found the written decree, "Let the _____ be rebuilt." (Ezra 6:3-5)

8. Darius wrote a letter saying, "Do not interfere. Let them rebuild the temple of _____ on its site." (Ezra 6:7)

9. When Nehemiah heard that the _____ of Jerusalem were in ruins, he sat down and wept. He mourned and fasted and _____ for many days. (Neh. 1:1-11)

10. The _____ saw that he was greatly troubled and asked him, "Why are you so sad?" So Nehemiah told him about the situation in _____ and asked permission to go and help. The king appointed him as governor of Judah and sent him there, accompanied by captains of the _____ and soldiers on horses. (Neh. 2:1-9) (Neh. 5:14)

11. The enemies of the Jews threatened to come and _____ the workers. Fear gripped their hearts, so they set up _____ to watch day and night. (Neh. 4:9-11)

12. Nehemiah spoke to the workers, "Don't be afraid. Remember the Lord is _____ and awesome. Fight for your brothers, your _____, your daughters, your wives and your _____." (Neh. 4:6-14)

13. The people continued working and it took only _____ days to complete the project. When their enemies and surrounding _____ heard about this achievement, they were _____ because they realized the work had been done with _____ help. (Neh. 6:15-16)

14. On a certain day, all the people assembled and Ezra read the _____ of God to them from morning until _____. They listened intently, worshiped the Lord and _____. (Neh. 8:1-8)

15. Nehemiah said, "This day is holy to the Lord. Do not _____ or weep. Go your way, eat the fat, _____ sweet wine, and send food to those who have none. Do not be grieved, for the _____ of the Lord is your strength." So the people went their way with great _____. (Neh. 8:10-12)

Crossword 35 – Returning to Jerusalem

Use these words:
army, carpenters, cedar, Darius, Ezra, fight, fox, glory, governor, Haggai, Joppa, Judah, Lebanon Nehemiah, noon, Persia, rebellious, ruins, stop, strength, treasurer, trouble, weapons, with

ACROSS
1 - The king's ___ counted all the precious items that had been taken out of the Temple.
3 - One king sent officers who forced the work on the temple to ___.
5 - Some families took ___ and used it to panel their own homes.
9 - God's prophet ___ preached, "Consider your ways!"
12 - Ezra read the Law of God to the people from morning until ___.
15 - The king of ___ said the Jews in his kingdom could go back and rebuild their temple.
16 - The non-Jewish people living near Jerusalem made ___ for those who came to rebuild.
18 - ___ was a scribe and priest who ministered to those who returned to rebuild Jerusalem.
20 - King Cyrus purchased cedar logs from ___.
21 - God said, "I am ___ you as I've always been."
22 - The builders kept their ___ with them while they worked.
23 - The Jews were accused of rebuilding a "___ and evil" city.

DOWN
2 - Nehemiah's king sent captains of the ___ and soldiers on horses to travel with him.
3 - "The joy of the Lord is your ___."
4 - ___ was a Jewish man who served in the court of the king of Persia.
6 - Nehemiah said, "___ for your brothers, sons, daughters, wives, and homes."
7 - The king paid masons and ___ to work on rebuilding the temple.
8 - Someone said, "Even a ___ could break down the stone wall those people built."
10 - The cedar logs were shipped to the seaport town of ___.
11 - King ___ searched in the archives and found the decree: "Let the temple be rebuilt."
13 - King Cyrus appointed Nehemiah to be ___ over Judah. (Neh. 5:14)
14 - Nehemiah mourned and fasted for days; then he asked the king if he could go to ___.
17 - "The 'Desire of Nations' will come and I will fill this temple with ___." (Hag. 2:7-9)
19 - "You live in cedar paneled houses while my house lies in ___!" (Hag. 1:4)

Storyboard 35 - Returning to Jerusalem

Section 1 - Time to Build

This first section is an easy narrative to tell. Draw some icons in the first box on the facing page to remember the sequence of events. It's best to draw many icons because of the many moving parts in this section.

Section 2 - Finishing the Temple

Draw five icons to help you remember the sequence of this section. They should represent:
- paneled houses
- common wood
- 'Desire of all the Nations'
- new king
- four years

Section 3 - Sending Nehemiah

Draw five icons that will help you remember the sequence of this section. They should represent:
- visitors from Judah
- told the king
- going to Judah
- met with leaders
- enemies

Section 4 - Finishing the Wall

There are more details in this section. Therefore, draw five more icons that will help you remember what happened. They should represent:
- halfway up
- threatened
- working with weapons
- fifty-two days
- reading the Law of God

Additional Learning Technique

This story includes several locations, so **Walk Around the Room** is another good way to learn it. Find locations representing these places:
- Persia
- Lebanon
- Judah
- Temple site
- people's homes
- broken down walls around Jerusalem
- king's court where Nehemiah lived
- place where Ezra read God's Law to the people

Drawing Storyboard 35 – Returning to Jerusalem

Using the boxes below, show the storyboard in pictures, symbols, or words.

Time to Build	Finishing the Temple
Sending Nehemiah	Finishing the Wall

Reflection – 35

- What was your favorite part of the story? Tell why.
  _____

- What did you learn about people from *Returning to Jerusalem?*
  _____

- What did you learn about God from *Returning to Jerusalem?*
  _____

Communication Activities
Communicate the story in your most enjoyable form of expression.

- **Art:** Paint (or draw) a picture of one of the scenes in this story.
- **Storytelling:** Write and tell a first-person story as if you are one of the common people who went back to Israel to rebuild the Temple and were still there to help rebuild the wall.
- **Storytelling:** "Tandem Telling" is where two people take turns telling the same story. Select someone else to join you, and practice telling this story in tandem. Once the two of you can easily get through the story, tell it to an audience.
- **Music:** Write a ballad with four verses.
    1) The people going back to rebuild the Temple
    2) The people using the cedar to panel their own houses
    3) The people building the walls of Jerusalem
    4) The nation rejoicing over completion of the walls
- **News Report:** Write several articles on this story as if it will appear in the ancient *Jerusalem Times*. Refer to the Scriptures *II Chronicles 36:21-23, Ezra 1-6, Haggai 1-2,* and *Nehemiah 1-13* for more details.
- **Poetry:** Write the entire story as a poem.
- **Scrapbook/Poster:** Find small pictures that illustrate each part of this story and display them on a poster.

Student has completed one or more of the communication activities.   Teacher initials _____

Banner or Bumper Sticker: Give the essence of this story in seven words or less.

Tell the story: To whom did you tell the story, and what was their response?

_____

_____

Group Discussion - 35

Returning to Jerusalem

1. God sent the prophet Haggai to challenge the people about their priorities. Tell of a time when someone helped you reevaluate your priorities.

2. The people were told to use common wood instead of cedar for the temple. Name a time when your feelings of being inadequate kept you from doing an important job.

3. The people took the responsibility of rebuilding the wall and divided the work among family teams. Tell of a time when you were a part of a team that divided up responsibilities in order to make a project successful.

4. The enemies of God's people mocked and insulted the workers. What is a good way we can handle ridicule when we're trying to accomplish something meaningful?

5. After hearing God's law, the people shared food and drink with those who had none. How can acts of generosity deepen community bonds and reflect God's love in practical ways?

Notes:

Introduction to Lesson 36

The story of Esther is set in the Persian Empire during the reign of King Ahasuerus (also known as Xerxes I). The Jewish people in Persia at this time were the ones that didn't go back to Jerusalem during the time of Ezra and Nehemiah.

The King of Persia hosted a lavish banquet in preparation for his upcoming invasion of Greece. His queen refused to dance for his drunken guests, so she was banished. Beautiful virgins were assembled, and they went through a time of purification in preparation for being presented to the king.

The story of Queen Esther takes place when King Ahasuerus returned in disgrace after losing his war with Greece. This loss weighed heavily on his mind, contributing to his sleepless nights and making him more susceptible to Haman's manipulation, which led to the decree to annihilate the Jewish people.

Lesson 36 ~ Esther
The Book of Esther

Esther was a beautiful young woman raised by her older cousin Mordecai. She was selected to be the new queen of Persia, and Mordecai warned her not to reveal that she was Jewish.

Soon after this, Mordecai discovered a plot to assassinate the king. He reported it, and the two guilty men were hanged. Mordecai's good deed was recorded in the official records.

Haman was the highest-ranking official in the government. People bowed to him when he walked by, that is, everyone except Mordecai. This enraged Haman, and he wanted to destroy Mordecai's entire race. Haman convinced the king to issue a decree ordering all the Jews to be killed on a certain date. Fear and panic swept throughout the land!

Mordecai told Esther about this decree and said, "Talk to the king and beg him to have mercy on your people."

Esther replied, "Approaching the king without an invitation is punishable by death unless he extends his golden scepter. "

Mordecai said, "Don't think that because you are in the king's palace you will escape . . . and who knows but that you have come to the kingdom for such a time as this?"

Esther sent a message back to Mordecai, "Tell everyone to fast for three days, then I'll go before the king, even though it is against the law. If I die, I die."

After three days, Esther put on her royal robes and stood where the king could see her from his throne. When he looked up, he was pleased and immediately held out his golden scepter. He said, "Tell me what you want, and I'll grant it."

Esther requested that the king and Haman attend a banquet she would prepare. He agreed. After the meal, the king asked her again, "What is your request so I can give it to you?" She replied, "Please come with Haman to another banquet tomorrow, and I'll tell you then."

Haman was thrilled about the invitation to both banquets, but again became furious when Mordecai refused to bow before him. That evening, Haman complained to his wife and friends about Mordecai's disrespect. They suggested he build a 75-foot gallows and then, the next morning, ask the king's permission to hang Mordecai on it.

That night, the king couldn't sleep and asked for a servant to read the royal records to him. He heard about Mordecai's role in saving his life and asked his servant, "What has been done to honor this man?"

"Nothing, my king."

"Nothing was done to reward him? Go into the court and see if anyone is there."

The servant found Haman standing there, waiting to see the king. The king brought him in and asked, "What should I do for a man I want to honor in a special way?"

Thinking he was about to be honored, Haman said, "Oh, my king. You should put your royal robe and crown on him. Place him on your horse and have your most noble official lead him through the streets shouting, 'This is what the king does for a man he wants to honor!'"

"Excellent," the king said. "Do all of this for Mordecai. Leave nothing out."

Haman was mortified as he carried out the king's orders, leading Mordecai through the streets with celebration. When it was all over, Haman went to the queen's second banquet.

After they ate, the king asked Esther, "Tell me what you want so I can give it to you." She pleaded, "Oh king, spare my life and the lives of my people. A man has plotted to destroy my entire race."

The king was shocked and demanded, "Who is this man?"

Esther pointed at Haman. "Our enemy is this wicked man."

Terrified and speechless, Haman could only listen as a servant added, "Haman built a gallows on which to hang Mordecai, the man who saved your life."

The king pointed to Haman and said, "Hang him on it!"

Haman was immediately taken out and executed on the gallows he had built. Then his position was given to Mordecai.

So the Jewish people were saved, and Mordecai became the highest-ranking official in the kingdom.

Search the Scriptures 36 ~ Esther
The Book of Esther

1. Esther was brought to the palace of the _____ of Persia along with many other young women. She was _____ and was chosen as the new _____. (2: 8,17)
2. Esther was an orphan, so her cousin, _____, took her and raised her as his own daughter. Mordecai told her _____ to tell anyone she was Jewish. (2:5-10)
3. In Mordecai's work, he discovered a plot to _____ the king. This was investigated and the two conspirators were hanged. It was recorded in the official record _____. (2:21-23)
4. Haman was _____ by the king, and everyone was required to _____ down to him. But Mordecai would not bow down or pay him honor. This made Haman _____. (3:1-6)
5. Haman went to the king and advised that all the Jews should be _____. The king said, "Do whatever seems good to you." So Haman put the decree in _____ and sent it out to the whole _____. This caused the whole city to be greatly troubled. (3:8-15)
6. Mordecai sent a message to _____ telling her to go to the _____, beg for mercy, and plead with him to spare her _____." Esther said, "Anyone who approaches the king without being _____ will be put to death unless the king extends the _____ scepter to them. (4:1-11)
7. Mordecai answered, "Do not think that because you are in the king's _____ you will escape . . . and who knows but that you have _____ to the kingdom for such a _____ as this?" (4:13-14)
8. Esther replied to Mordecai: "You and all the Jews, fast for _____ days and nights. I and my attendants will also _____. Then I will _____ to the king, and if I perish, I _____." (4:15-16)
9. After _____ days, Esther went to the king. He held out his scepter and asked, "What is your request?" "Please let the king and Haman, come to a _____ I have prepared today." So they came. (5:1-4)
10. _____ the meal, the king again asked Esther, "What is your _____? Esther replied, "I ask that you and Haman come to my banquet _____ and I will tell you my request." (5:6-8)
11. Haman went out feeling _____. But when he passed by Mordecai, who once again refused to bow down, Haman was filled with _____! He went home and told his _____ and friends. They suggested he build a _____ and have Mordecai executed on it. So Haman had it made. (5:9-14)
12. That night the king couldn't _____, so he asked that the palace record _____ be brought in and _____ to him. It told about Mordecai having discovered the plot to _____ the king. He asked, "_____ has been done to honor Mordecai for this?" They said, "_____." (6:1-3)
13. The king asked, "_____ is in the court?" They said, "_____ is in the court." "Bring him in." (6:4-5)
14. The king asked Haman, "_____ should be done for a man the king wishes to _____?" Haman thought of himself. He said, "Put a royal _____ on him and set him on one of the king's _____. _____ him through the city shouting, 'This is what is done for the man the king wants to honor!'" (6:5-10)
15. The king said, "Do this for Mordecai the _____. Haman obeyed the king's orders and then mournfully went _____ to get ready for the _____. (6:11-14)
16. After they had _____, the king again asked, "What is your petition?" Esther answered, "Please save the lives of _____ and my _____. For we have been sold and are destined to be _____. The king asked Esther, "_____ is he and _____ is the man who has dared to do such a thing?"
17. Esther said, "Our _____ is this wicked Haman." Then Haman was _____! (7:1-7)
18. The king was enraged! One of the _____ said, "There is a _____ set up by Haman's house. He made it for Mordecai." The king said, "_____ him on it." So they did. (7:8-10)

Crossword 36 – Esther

Use these words:
banquet, beautiful, book, destroyed, Esther, gallows, Haman, happy, horses, Jewish, job, kill, kingdom Mordecai, nothing, orphan, people, Persia, petition, queen, record, scepter, sleep, three

ACROSS

3 - Mordecai rode on one of the king's ___.
5 - Esther was a very ___ woman.
6 - Esther begged, "Please save the lives of me and my ___."
10 - Esther asked the Jews to fast for ___ days and three nights.
11 - Mordecai told Esther not to tell anyone she was ___.
12 - One night, the king could not ___.
16 - When Haman was hanged, his ___ was given to Mordecai.
17 - Twice, Esther invited the king and Haman to a ___.
18 - The king promoted ___, and everyone was supposed to bow down to him.
19 - ___ raised Esther; she was like a daughter to him.
20 - Esther was married to the king of ___.
21 - "Who knows but that you have come to the ___ for such a time as this?"

DOWN

1 - Haman had a ___ set up by his house.
2 - Mordecai discovered a plot to ___ the king.
3 - Haman felt very ___ as he left the first banquet.
4 - The king held out his golden ___ to Esther.
6 - The king asked Esther, "What is your ___?"
7 - Esther was an ___.
8 - Haman wanted all the Jews in the kingdom to be ___.
9 - The king of Persia was looking for a new ___.
13 - The king asked, "What was done to honor him?" The answer: "___."
14 - ___ was brought to the king's palace along with many other young women.
15 - Mordecai's good deed was written down in the palace ___ book.
17 - The king asked that someone read to him from the ___ of official records.

Storyboard 36 - Esther

The only difficulty to learning this story is that it has many moving parts. Therefore, it is important to remember what comes next. To do this, break the story into four sections and draw icons or create hand gestures that will help you remember everything that happened in that section.

Section 1 - Becoming Queen
In this section, draw icons or create hand gestures that represent the following:
1) the selection of a new queen
2) hearing about the assassination plot
3) the highest-ranking official
4) the decree to kill the Jews
5) "If I die, I die"

Practice telling this section until it becomes easy.

Section 2 - Banquets
In this section, draw icons or create hand gestures that represent the following:
1) the king seeing his queen
2) attending the first banquet
3) invitation to a second banquet
4) joy turning to anger.

Practice telling this section until it becomes easy.

Section 3 - Sleepless Night
In this section, draw icons or create hand gestures that represent the following:
1) the king can't sleep
2) how shall I show honor?
3) find Mordecai

Practice telling this section until it becomes easy.

Section 4 - Saved from Destruction
In this section, draw icons or create hand gestures that represent the following:
1) "tell me what you want"
2) "who is this man that dared to do such a thing?"
3) replacing Haman with Mordecai

Practice telling this section until it becomes easy.

Drawing Storyboard 36 – Esther

Using the boxes below, show the storyboard in pictures, symbols, or words

Becoming Queen	*Banquets*
Sleepless Night	*Saved from Destruction*

Reflection – 36

- What was your favorite part of the story? Tell why.
  _____

- What did you learn about people from the story of *Esther*?
  _____

- What did you learn about God from the story of *Esther*?
  _____

Communication Activities
Communicate the story in your most enjoyable form of expression.

- **Art:** Paint (or draw) a picture of Esther going before the king, or of Haman begging Esther to have mercy on him, or of Haman leading Mordecai through the streets.
- **Storytelling:** Read the book of Esther in the Bible and identify the various parts that are not included in the story in this book. Select one and add it to the story you have learned.
- **Impromptu Drama:** Two people go to a far-off city to meet a friend in a Persian coffee shop. The friend asks for interesting news from the capital city. The two people excitedly tell their friend about the king, his queen, Haman, and Mordecai. As they tell what happened, the friend keeps asking for more details. Answer these impromptu questions even if you have to make things up.
- **Music:** Craft a song that retells this story in music.
- **Poetry:** Retell the story in poetry.
- **News Report:** Write an article of this story as if it is from an ancient Persian newspaper. Read *The book of Esther* for more details.
- **Research:** Study and report on King Ahasuerus (Xerxes I) and the war he lost in Greece.

Student has completed one or more of the communication activities.   Teacher initials _____

Banner or Bumper Sticker: Give the essence of this story in seven words or less.

[   ]

Tell the story to an individual or a group. To whom did you tell the story, and what was their response?
_____
_____

Group Discussion - 36

Esther

1. Mordecai refused to bow to Haman, knowing it would be dangerous. Share a time when you had to be true to your faith, even though it was not popular.

2. Haman let his anger toward Mordecai deteriorate into unchecked hatred. How can we prevent this from happening in our own lives?

3. Mordecai told Esther she was in a position to save her people. Tell about a time when you were uniquely positioned to make a difference for others? Possibly you have seen this in someone else.

4. What does this story teach us about the importance of courage and taking risks for what is right?

5. What qualities do you admire about Esther? What do you admire about Mordecai?

NOTES:

Test 28 ~ Solomon

____ 1. God appeared to Solomon in ____ and said, "Ask what I shall give you."
        a. the Temple   b. a field   c. a dream

____ 2. Solomon asked for ____ to rule the Lord's people.
        a. wise counselors   b. a book of laws   c. an understanding heart

____ 3. God was ____ with Solomon's request.
        a. surprised   b. pleased   c. disappointed

____ 4. God said he would also give Solomon ____.
        a. mercy and truth   b. riches and honor   c. sons and daughters

____ 5. God said if Solomon would walk in the ways of the Lord, he would ____ his days.
        a. lengthen   b. shorten   c. brighten

____ 6. Two ____ came to King Solomon and told him their stories.
        a. men   b. women   c. servants

____ 7. They each had a ____, but one was dead and the other was alive.
        a. calf   b. lamb   c. child

____ 8. They both claimed the ____ one as their own.
        a. dead   b. living   c. bigger

____ 9. Solomon commanded that the baby be ____.
        a. divided   b. sold   c. given away

____ 10. All Israel saw that the ____ of God was in Solomon.
        a. face   b. wisdom   c. kindness

____ 11. His ____ spread throughout all the surrounding nations.
        a. fame   b. family   c. army

____ 12. Kings from other nations came to hear Solomon ____.
        a. read   b. sing   c. speak

____ 13. Solomon began to build the Temple ____ years after the Israelites came out of Egypt.
        a. 240   b. 360   c. 480

____ 14. The inside walls of the temple were made of ____.
        a. cedar   b. pine   c. oak

____ 15. The inner sanctuary was covered with pure ____.
        a. diamonds   b. onyx   c. gold

____ 16. Solomon's Temple took ____ years to build.
        a. three   b. seven   c. twelve

____ 17. The priests brought the ____ from the tabernacle and set it in the Most Holy Place.
        a. altar   b. Ark of God   c. incense

____ 18. When the priests came out of the Most Holy Place, ____ filled the house of the Lord.
        a. lightning   b. thunder   c. a cloud

____ 19. Solomon wrote 3,000 proverbs and more than 1,000 ____.
        a. songs   b. books   c. letters

____ 20. God warned that if his people forsook him, he would remove himself from the ____.
        a. Temple   b. city gate   c. city wall

(5 points each question)   SCORE _____

Test 29 – Naaman

Matching

____ 1. The King of Syria   a. Who had a young Israelite girl as a servant?

____ 2. The King of Israel   b. Who said Naaman could be cured by the prophet in Samaria?

____ 3. Naaman   c. Who wrote a letter to the king of Israel?

____ 4. Naaman's wife   d. He said, "I'm not God! I can't cure people from leprosy!"

____ 5. Naaman's servants   e. He said, "Go and wash seven times in the Jordan River."

____ 6. Gehazi   f. Who advised Naaman to follow the prophet's instructions?

____ 7. A young Israelite girl   g. Who promised to worship only the God of Israel?

____ 8. The prophet Elisha   h. He said, "I will not accept a gift from you."

____ 9. Elisha's messenger who met Naaman at the door   i. He said, "I went nowhere."

Multiple Choice

____ 10. Naaman was the ____ in Syria.
    a. crown prince   b. army commander   c. high priest

____ 11. Naaman had a serious problem; he was ____.
    a. crippled   b. blind   c. a leper

____ 12. What did Naaman take with him to Samaria?
    a. his wife and son   b. ten camels   c. his servants, a letter, and many gifts

____ 13. The King of Israel thought that the King of Syria was trying to ____.
    a. trick him   b. start a quarrel with him   c. take over his country

____ 14. Naaman said the rivers of ____ were better than the rivers in Israel.
    a. Damascus   b. Alexandria   c. Jericho

____ 15. What was Naaman's skin like after he was healed?
    a. expensive silk   b. as white as snow   c. the flesh of a young child

____ 16. Naaman asked Elisha to give him as much ____ as two mules could carry.
    a. soil   b. fruit   c. gold

____ 17. Gehazi thought that Naaman should have ____.
    a. paid something   b. apologized   c. stayed in Samaria longer

____ 18. After Naaman started home, Gehazi chased after him and asked for ____.
    a. diamonds and rubies   b. horses and donkeys   c. silver and clothing

____ 19. Gehazi said they needed the things for their visitors who were ____.
    a. a family in need   b. two young prophets   c. government officials

____ 20. Gehazi was punished by ____.
    a. losing his job   b. getting leprosy   c. being put in stocks

(5 points each question)   SCORE _____

Test 30 - Four Lepers

Multiple Choice

____ 1. What city was besieged by the Syrian army?
    a. Jerusalem   b. Samaria   c. Jericho

____ 2. Who walked along the top of the city wall?
    a. prophet   b. priest   c. king

____ 3. Who cried out asking for help?
    a. the lepers   b. a woman   c. a child

____ 4. What was the disaster inside the city?
    a. famine   b. fire   c. flood

____ 5. The prophet predicted the price of ____ would drop drastically.
    a. food   b. silver   c. livestock

____ 6. God caused the Syrian army to hear the sound of ____.
    a. explosions   b. thunder   c. horses and chariots

____ 7. Who did the lepers find in the Syrian camp?
    a. no one   b. soldiers who were injured   c. the wives and children

____ 8. What did the two horsemen find on the ground?
    a. dead bodies   b. only ashes   c. supplies and equipment

____ 9. Who was trampled at the city gate?
    a. the four lepers   b. the king's chief adviser   c. the gatekeepers

Matching Quotations: Who said it?

Answers may be used more than once

____ 10. "Help me!"

____ 11. "What is your problem?"

____ 12. "May God strike me down if the head of Elisha remains on his shoulders by the end of this day."

____ 13. "Our murdering king has sent a guard to take off my head."

____ 14. "Tomorrow about this time, flour and barley will be sold for just shekels."

____ 15. "That couldn't happen if God himself should make windows in heaven!"

____ 16. "You will see it with your own eyes, but you will not eat any of it."

____ 17. "Why are we just sitting here dying of hunger?"

____ 18. "Let's go into the camp of the Syrians."

____ 19. "We are not doing right."

____ 20. "The Syrian army is hiding out of sight, just waiting for us to come out of the city."

a. the four lepers

b. a woman

c. Elisha

d. the king

e. the king's chief adviser

(5 points each question)   SCORE _____

Test 31 – Jonah

Matching Places

____ 1. Israel

____ 2. Joppa

____ 3. Tarshish

____ 4. on a pile of ashes

____ 5. lower part of the ship

____ 6. belly of the fish

____ 7. the shore

____ 8. Nineveh

____ 9. under a shelter on the east side of the city

a. seaport town

b. home country of Jonah

c. place the Lord sent Jonah to go and preach

d. place where Jonah was sleeping

e. place where the king sat to show his repentance

f. where Jonah was heading — opposite direction of Nineveh

g. place where Jonah submitted to God's will

h. where Jonah sat to watch what would happen

i. where the fish vomited up Jonah

Matching Quotations: Who said it?

____ 10. "Go to Nineveh and preach."

____ 11. "Get up and pray to your god."

____ 12. "Who are you and what have you done?"

____ 13. "I serve the Lord God who made the sea and dry ground."

____ 14. "What should we do to make the storm stop?"

____ 15. "Throw me overboard!"

____ 16. "Please forgive us for what we are about to do."

____ 17. "I will do what you want me to do."

____ 18. "God is going to destroy this city in 40 days!"

____ 19. "Maybe God will change his mind and allow us to live."

____ 20. "That's exactly why I didn't want to come here."

Answers may be used more than once

a. God

b. Jonah

c. the king

d. the ship captain

e. the sailors

(5 points each question)   SCORE _____

Test 32 – The King of Assyria

Matching People

____ 1. Assyrian army commander

____ 2. Isaiah

____ 3. Sennacherib

____ 4. Hezekiah

____ 5. Pharaoh

a. King of Judah

b. King of Assyria

c. King of Egypt

d. prophet of God

e. person who met with Hezekiah's men outside the wall

Multiple Choice

____ 6. The Assyrian army commander told King Hezekiah's men, "____ told me to destroy you."
 a. My king b. Your priest c. The Lord

____ 7. Hezekiah's palace officers didn't want the ____ to hear and understand such alarming words.
 a. children who were playing b. women drawing water c. men on the wall

____ 8. After that, the Assyrian commander spoke ____.
 a. very quietly b. very loudly c. in a different language

____ 9. He told the people, "Do not ____ Hezekiah when he says, 'The Lord will deliver us.'"
 a. hurt b. believe c. resist

____ 10. When Hezekiah heard this, he tore his clothes, put on sackcloth, and went to the ____.
 a. city gate b. town square c. House of the Lord

____ 11. He sent a message to the prophet Isaiah asking him to ____.
 a. come and visit b. pray for them c. speak to the Assyrians

____ 12. Isaiah sent a message back saying "Don't be ____."
 a. afraid b. deceived c. proud

____ 13. God caused the army commander to hear a rumor and ____ his own land.
 a. destroy b. flee from c. return to

____ 14. The King of Assyria invaded many nations and ____ their gods made of wood and stone.
 a. burned b. carried away c. worshiped

____ 15. King Hezekiah received a letter from the king of ____.
 a. Assyria b. Babylon c. Egypt

____ 16. The words of Sennacherib showed ____ for the living God.
 a. respect b. disrespect c. fear

____ 17. Hezekiah wanted God to protect Jerusalem so all the world would know that ____.
 a. Assyria was wicked b. God's people were faithful c. the Lord alone is God

____ 18. God said he would defend Jerusalem for his own sake and for his servant ____ sake.
 a. Hezekiah's b. David's c. Isaiah's

____ 19. After his soldiers died, Sennacherib went home to ____.
 a. Nineveh b. Jerusalem c. Egypt

____ 20. Sennacherib was killed by two of ____.
 a. his sons b. Hezekiah's men c. God's angels

(5 points each question) SCORE _____

Test 33 – Jeremiah

____ 1. When God called Jeremiah to preach, he answered ____.
    a. "I will obey you."   b. "I am not worthy."   c. "I don't want this job."

____ 2. God said, "I chose you for this job ____."
    a. because I love you   b. before you were born   c. over all your brothers

____ 3. God told Jeremiah to go to ____.
    a. the gate of the city   b. the potter's house   c. the House of the Lord

____ 4. Jeremiah spoke to the rulers of Judah with a clay jar in his hands. Then he ____.
    a. showed off its beauty   b. poured them a drink   c. threw it on the ground

____ 5. The jar symbolized what God would do with ____.
    a. the city of Jerusalem   b. the priests   c. the leaders of Judah

____ 6. The priest had Jeremiah ____.
    a. sent to the king   b. honored   c. beaten

____ 7. Jeremiah told the priest, "God has changed your name to '____.'
    a. majesty   b. terror   c. fearful

____ 8. God told Jeremiah to write a book about the ____ of Jerusalem.
    a. future   b. history   c. beauty

____ 9. When the book was done, Jeremiah's scribe went to the Temple and read it to the ____.
    a. people   b. foreigners   c. children

____ 10. The government officials took the book and read it to the king, and he ____.
    a. worshiped the Lord   b. proclaimed a fast   c. burned the book

____ 11. The Lord told Jeremiah to write another book ____.
    a. with a different title   b. the same as before   c. twice as long

____ 12. Jeremiah told the people of Judah, "Babylon will come and ____ this city."
    a. make peace with   b. surrender to   c. destroy

____ 13. Babylon will take you ____.
    a. into captivity   b. to see far-off lands   c. to new heights of culture

____ 14. You will be away from your homeland for ____ years.
    a. seven   b. seventy   c. seven hundred

____ 15. The Babylonian army came and took more than ten thousand ____.
    a. pieces of silver   b. captives   c. golden candlesticks

____ 16. They left behind only the ____.
    a. poorest people   b. priests   c. soldiers

____ 17. On their last invasion, the Babylonians burned all the buildings and broke down the ____.
    a. walls of Jerusalem   b. trees in the fields   c. ships in the harbor

____ 18. In Jeremiah's vision were two baskets of ____.
    a. fish   b. figs   c. bread

____ 19. God promised to watch over the people in captivity and give them ____.
    a. great riches   b. contentment   c. a desire to know God

____ 20. God warned that if his people forsook him, he would remove himself from ____.
    a. the Temple   b. nature   c. them forever

(5 points each question)   SCORE _____

Test 34 – Daniel

Matching

____ 1. Jerusalem

____ 2. An upstairs room

____ 3. The lion's den

____ 4. "Oh, King, live forever!"

____ 5. The royal court of Nebuchadnezzar

____ 6. The royal court of Darius

____ 7. The law King Darius was persuaded to write by evil men

____ 8. The new law King Darius wrote to replace the bad one.

a. place where Daniel served as a young captive

b. place where Daniel served as an older man

c. place where Daniel went to pray

d. place where Daniel was put as a punishment

e. "No one can pray to anyone except King Darius."

f. Traditional words to greet a king

g. "Everyone must reverence Daniel's God."

h. Babylonians conquered this city and took many young men captive

Multiple Choice

____ 9. Daniel's home town was ____.
    a. Jericho   b. Jerusalem   c. Nineveh

____ 10. Daniel was in Babylon because ____.
    a. he was visiting there   b. he went to find work   c. he was captured and taken there

____ 11. While in Babylon, his housing was provided by ____.
    a. the king   b. the priests   c. the military

____ 12. Daniel did not want to eat the food offered to him because it ____.
    a. tasted strange   b. was spoiled   c. went against God's law

____ 13. Daniel and his friends determined that they would not ____.
    a. offend the king   b. defile themselves   c. cooperate

____ 14. The young men were trained in ____ for three years.
    a. sports   b. music   c. language and literature

____ 15. After three years, Daniel and his friends were judged ten times ____ than the other 'wise men.'
    a. weaker   b. fatter   c. better

____ 16. Later in life Daniel became a top administrator under King ____.
    a. Darius   b. Solomon   c. Ahab

____ 17. The other administrators' purpose in convincing the king to make a law was to ____.
    a. honor the king   b. benefit everyone   c. get Daniel in trouble

____ 18. The law said no one could pray to anyone except ____ for thirty days.
    a. Baal   b. Darius   c. Zeus

____ 19. When Daniel heard about the law, he continued to kneel and pray in his room ____.
    a. three times a day   b. only after sunset   c. only before dawn

____ 20. God sent his angel to ____.
    a. shut the lions' mouths   b. make the lions sick   c. make the lions sleep

(5 points each question)   SCORE _____

Test 35 – Returning to Jerusalem

Matching Quotes

____ 1. Cyrus, king of Persia

____ 2. God

____ 3. Jewish people

____ 4. The prophet Haggai

____ 5. Nehemiah's king

____ 6. Nehemiah

____ 7. Ezra

____ 8. enemies of the Jews who were rebuilding the Temple

____ 9. enemies of the Jews who were rebuilding the walls of Jerusalem

a. "Consider your ways!"

b. "Why are you so sad?"

c. "This isn't a good time to build the Temple."

d. "They are building that rebellious and evil city."

e. "I am with you as I've always been."

f. "Fight for your brothers, your sons, your daughters, your wives, and your homes!"

g. "Their stone wall will fall down even if a fox goes up on it."

h. "The Jews in my kingdom are free to go and rebuild the Temple."

i. "The joy of the Lord is your strength."

Multiple Choice

____ 10. King Cyrus ordered the neighbors of people returning to Jerusalem give them ____.
   a. money and supplies   b. encouragement   c. horses for travel

____ 11. King Cyrus sent many ____ to Jerusalem with the people going there.
   a. bags of grain   b. fresh vegetables   c. items that belonged in the temple

____ 12. The non-Jewish people who lived in Judah were ____ about the Jews who were returning.
   a. happy   b. unhappy   c. indifferent

____ 13. The people in Judah used ____ to communicate with the king in Persia.
   a. runners   b. personal visits   c. letters

____ 14. When work on the temple was forced to stop, people took ____ from the building site.
   a. boulders   b. cedar   c. mortar

____ 15. Nehemiah was appointed to be the ____ of Judah.
   a. governor   b. priest   c. military commander

____ 16. The wall-builders kept their ____ with them while they worked.
   a. food supply   b. weapons   c. servants

____ 17. ____ paid the masons and carpenters for their work in rebuilding the Temple.
   a. Nehemiah   b. Haggai   c. King Cyrus

____ 18. ____ read the Law of God to the people.
   a. Haggai   b. Ezra   c. Nehemiah

____ 19. It took ____ years for the temple to be rebuilt.
   a. four   b. forty   c. four hundred

____ 20. It took ____ days for the walls of Jerusalem to be rebuilt.
   a. forty-two   b. fifty-two   c. sixty-two

(5 points each question)   SCORE _____

Test 36 – Esther

Multiple Choice

____ 1. Esther was like a ____ to Mordecai.
    a. mother   b. daughter   c. sister

____ 2. What kind of position did Haman have under the Persian king?
    a. second in command   b. household servant   c. one of the king's wise men

____ 3. What made Haman furious?
    a. people being lazy   b. children asking questions   c. someone not bowing down to him

____ 4. How did Esther feel about going to talk to the king?
    a. confident   b. worried   c. eager

Matching Quotations: Who said it?

Answers may be used more than once

____ 5. "Don't tell anyone you are Jewish."

____ 6. "Let a decree be written that all the Jewish people shall be destroyed on a certain day."

____ 7. "Do whatever seems good to you."

____ 8. "You must talk to the king and plead with him to save your people."

____ 9. "Anyone who approaches the king without being invited will be put to death unless the king extends his golden scepter."

____ 10. "Who knows but that you have come to the kingdom for such a time as this?"

____ 11. "Tell all the Jews to fast for three days and three nights. Then I will go to the king, and if I perish, I perish."

____ 12. "What is your petition?"

____ 13. "Let the king and Haman come to a banquet I have prepared."

____ 14. "Make a gallows and ask the king to have Mordecai hanged on it."

____ 15. "What has been done to honor Mordecai for this deed?"

____ 16. "Nothing."

____ 17. "This is what the king does for a man he wants to honor."

____ 18. "Oh, king, please save the lives of me and my people!"

____ 19. "There is a gallows set up by Haman's house."

____ 20. "Hang him on it!"

a. King of Persia

b. Mordecai

c. Esther

d. a servant

e. Haman

f. Haman's wife and friends

(5 points each question)   SCORE _____

Our Mission

Sharing the story of God for discipleship, using all the stories of the Bible.

Our Websites

BibleTelling.org - BibleTelling news, events, and services, including Holy Land Seminars, Training, and FREE download of *All the Stories of the Bible*

BTStories.com - free online access to audio, video, text, timeline, map, and insights for *All the Stories of the Bible*

LanguageOlympics.org - Literacy and ESL training using Bible stories

Story-of-the-Day Subscription

Receive an e-mail each weekday with links to the video, audio, and written narrative of the Story-of-the-Day.

E-mail your subscription request to: info@BibleTelling.com

Mobile App

Search for "BT Stories" in the Apple, Android, and Windows app stores.

Contact

E-mail: info@BibleTelling.com

Made in the USA
Monee, IL
15 April 2025

15813781R00057